AGAIN WITH
REJOICING

BRINGING IN
SHEAVES

WITH
HIM

SYLVIA PANKHURST

Artist and Crusader

SYLVIA PANKHURST

Artist and Crusader

An Intimate Portrait by
Richard Pankhurst

PADDINGTON PRESS LTD
NEW YORK AND LONDON

Library of Congress Cataloging in Publication Data
Pankhurst, Richard Keir Pethick, 1927–
    Sylvia Pankhurst, artist and crusader.

    Includes bibliographical references.
    1. Pankhurst, Estelle Sylvia, 1882–1960.   2. Femin-
ists—Great Britain—Biography.   3. Women artists—
Great Britain—Biography.   1. Pankhurst, Estelle Sylvia,
1882–1960.   11. Title.
HQ1595.P34P36   324′.3′0924 [B]   79–11668
ISBN 0 448 22840 8 (U.S. and Canada only)
ISBN 0 7092 0628 3

Published in association with Virago Ltd.
Filmset in England by Tradespools Ltd., Frome, Somerset
Color separations by Starf Photolito, Rome, Italy
Printed and bound in Italy by Poligrafici Calderara
Designed by Sandra Shafee and Pete Pengilley
Endpapers: Prince's Skating Rink Exhibition, May 1909.
Canvas at the far end of the skating rink.

In the United States
PADDINGTON PRESS
Distributed by
GROSSET & DUNLAP
In the United Kingdom
PADDINGTON PRESS
In Canada
Distributed by
RANDOM HOUSE OF CANADA LTD.
In Southern Africa
Distributed by
ERNEST STANTON (PUBLISHERS) (PTY.) LTD.
In Australia and New Zealand
Distributed by
A.H. & A.W. REED

CONTENTS

ACKNOWLEDGMENTS   6

INTRODUCTION   7

1 Childhood; Political and Artistic Influence   9

2 School; the Independent Labour Party; Keir Hardie; the Manchester School of Art   23

3 Venice; Pankhurst Hall, Salford; the Founding of the WSPU   30

4 The Royal College of Art; Austin Spare; Early Suffragette Activity   46

5 Beginnings of Women's Militancy in Manchester and London; Artist or Social Reformer?   55

6 Two Imprisonments in Holloway; Prison Sketches; Drawings for the WSPU   63

7 Studying and Sketching Women's Work in Northern England and Scotland; Electioneering for the WSPU   75

8 Increased Suffragette Militancy; WSPU Designs and Banners; Decorations for the Prince's Skating Rink   100

9 Escalating Militancy; Oberammergau; the United States; Late Paintings   124

10 The East End; Hunger, Thirst and Sleep Strikes; Forcible Feeding; the "Cat and Mouse" Act   159

11 The East London Federation of Suffragettes; the *Woman's Dreadnought*; Forcing the Prime Minister to Receive a Deputation; the End of an Artistic Career   171

12 The First World War; the Rise of Fascism; Author and Mother; the Italo-Ethiopian War; Emigration to Addis Ababa   179

SOURCES   221

DETAILS OF WORKS   224

✨ ACKNOWLEDGMENTS

I would like to thank first and foremost Tom Evans, a scholar and artist who took the majority of the photographs here reproduced, made careful notes of any inscriptions, and suggested a tentative chronology for the pictures.

I would also acknowledge my debt to Victoria Moger of the Museum of London who shared with me her considerable knowledge of the literature of the women's movement, traced a number of my mother's Suffragette designs, and made photographs available; also to her colleague, Valerie Cumming, who provided details of a banner preserved in the museum, one of the finest in Britain.

Thanks are due to the International Institute of Social History in Amsterdam for kindly furnishing photographs of paintings and drawings which I deposited there, and to W.H.Van der Linden who provided details on them.

I am specially grateful to Alicia Percival who most kindly provided me with two of my mother's paintings here reproduced, and to Frank Dane, who gave me a third, to Ivy Tims who returned to me the portrait by Austin O. Spare which my mother had given her two decades earlier. I am also indebted to Malcolm and Dorothy O'Brien who permitted the photographing of the numerous pictures in their possession; to their daughter Molly Cook for an additional one they had given her; to Pat Romero Curtin for allowing the photographing of a study she had recently acquired; and to David Mitchell for a photograph of a group of Suffragettes.

Among those who encouraged and assisted me in the research I would record my gratitude to Roxane Arnold, Jill Craigie and Enid GouldenBach; Elisabeth McGrath of the Warburg Institute; Jean M.Ayton, Archivist of the Manchester Central Library; Irene Wagner, Librarian of the Labour Party; Elizabeth Cuthbert, Deputy Registrar of the Royal Archives at Windsor Castle; J.H.Shirt, Local History Librarian of the City of Salford; and David Doughan and Amanda Golby, both of the Fawcett Library, City of London Polytechnic.

I would record my thanks to Ursula Owen, of Virago, and Emma Dally, of Paddington Press, both of whom read the text and made valuable suggestions.

The work also owes much to my wife, Rita, who helped to conceive many aspects of it.

M<small>Y MOTHER, SYLVIA PANKHURST</small>, is variously remembered as a Suffragette and feminist; as a woman who worked for social betterment and Socialism in the East End of London and elsewhere; and as an anti-Fascist who espoused the cause of Ethiopia at the time of Mussolini's invasion of that country in 1935. Her first intentions, however, were to become an artist. After studying art in Manchester, she spent a summer and autumn painting in Venice before attending the Royal College of Art in London. Though yearning for the life of an artist she was soon drawn away by her need to participate in the militant movement for women's suffrage.

In this study I have attempted to introduce her artistic work – up to now scarcely known – and to set it in the context of her eventful life, the last quarter of which it was my privilege, as her son, to witness and share with her.

The drawings, paintings and decorations here reproduced, have for the most part never been exhibited or published. Produced within no more than a decade, they fall into several distinct categories. There are early sketches by a young and relatively carefree English art student in Italy in 1902; detailed studies of women industrial and agricultural workers by an idealistic young artist who travelled all over Britain in 1907 to paint and describe as faithfully as she could their monotonous and backbreaking activities; designs, badges, banners and decorations of all kinds, in Pre-Raphaelite style, mainly reproduced between 1908 and 1909, for the fast growing Suffragette movement; and studies, largely of the female form, conceived around 1910 by a more experienced artist about to abandon paint-brush and palette for increasingly active participation in the women's movement. There are also a few prison sketches, a self-portrait and two portrait studies of her old friend Keir Hardie, the veteran Socialist and founder of the Labour party, and several designs for posters and other decorations. Though most of the art here presented is, in the nature of things, immature, the representation of early twentieth-century women workers, which I have sought to supplement by her own accounts of the occupations depicted, and the Suffragette designs and decorations, may be of interest to social historians of the time.

After touching upon some of the influences that moulded my mother's artistic ideals and conceptions I have tried to examine the factors that drew her agonisingly from what she regarded as the cherished world of art to what seemed to her the bleaker one of politics.

I have also tried to trace her later life, concentrating on the last quarter of the century, partly because it is the only period in which I can speak from personal observation, but also because it illustrates the kind of political and social preoccupations to which in the final analysis she gave first priority.

RICHARD PANKHURST
London, 1979

✣ 1 Childhood;
Political and Artistic Influence

M Y MOTHER, ESTELLE SYLVIA PANKHURST, was born on May 5, 1882, at 1 Drayton Gardens, Old Trafford. She was called Estelle by her mother and Sylvia by her father, but, as she afterwards recalled, from an early age "the minx would respond only to the latter" by which she was in consequence always known.[1]

Recalling her childhood at "Old Trafford", as they spoke of it in the nursery, she was later to recall it with the eye of an artist. She could bring back to her mind : "Only a soft, grey dimness ; figures of people unrecognisable and flickering ; the dazzling light of windows, filtering through the prevailing haze, and the deeper shade of some half-open door." That, "overhung with a sense of vain and restless search to remember further", was all that she could discern.[2]

At about the age of two, Sylvia and her elder sister Christabel, born in September 1880, were taken by their father and mother to stay in the house of their maternal grandparents, Robert and Jane Goulden, at Seedley Cottage, Pendleton, on the Salford side of Manchester. There two further Pankhurst children were born – a boy, Henry Francis, in February 1884, and a third girl, Adela, in May 1885.

Of her childhood at Seedley Cottage, Sylvia was to write half a century later : "I remember the great gardens, and the large rooms with their heavy Victorian furniture, the big dining table I was running round when I got dizzy and had that fall into the fire, one mark of which I bear on my arm today. That accident made me the pet of four aunts and five uncles, kind youths and maidens, all of them ; my mother was second of the ten." Looking back across the years she also recalled a "wonderful Christmas pantomime" produced by her aunts and uncles in which she was given the part of Cinderella, and Christabel that of the prince. Sylvia's dress for the ball came out of a monster Christmas cracker and was of pink tulle with a stiff little ballet skirt. She rode on an elephant composed of two of her uncles. These were her "highlights of childhood's ecstasy, remembered because in the nursery so often recounted".[3]

Everything at Seedley, she recalled, was "on a grand scale". Her grand-mother was a typical old-fashioned housewife of the mid-Victorian era, working among the maids in a household producing its own butter and bread, jams, pickles and cakes, where laundering was an art, and where a sewing woman came in for garment-making at appropriate seasons.[4]

The dominant influence on Sylvia throughout her life was that of her father, Richard Marsden Pankhurst, of whom she always spoke with reverence, and whose portrait and framed election addresses hung on the walls of her study for as long as I can remember. It is no doubt likewise significant that she sometimes used the *nom de plume* Richard Marsden and was to call her only son Richard.

Richard Pankhurst, who was twenty years older than his wife Emmeline, was a lawyer, popularly known in his circle as "the Doctor" because he held a doctorate in law from the University of London. He was the author of numerous articles on international law and jurisprudence. A prominent member of the Manchester Literary and Philosophical Association, and of the National Association for the Promotion of Social Science, an organisation involved in all aspects of social reform, he was also a member of the Royal Statistical Society and the Society for the Reform and Codification of the Law of Nations.

Dr. Pankhurst, a friend and admirer of the old Chartist leader Ernest Jones, and of the liberal utilitarian John Stuart Mill, was a Liberal and a Republican, who had worked for the return to power of Gladstone, and had been active in the establishment of evening classes for working people. An early supporter of women's enfranchisement, in the late 1860s he had drafted the first unsuccessful women's suffrage bill, as well as the amendment which had given women the franchise in municipal elections. In 1883, the year after Sylvia's birth, he had stood as an independent candidate for Manchester, but, demanding as he did universal suffrage for both men and women, the nationalisation of land, the abolition of the House of Lords, the disestablish-ment of the Church, and home rule for Ireland, it was scarcely surprising that he was not elected.

Concern for what he considered the public good did not prevent the Doctor from taking a keen interest in his young wife and family. Of the latter he was often to say, "My children are the four pillars of my house!" though to them he would no less frequently observe, earnestly yet kindly, "If you do not work for others you will not have been worth the upbringing." Another of

Richard Marsden
Pankhurst, *c.* 1896.

his sayings was: "Life is nothing without enthusiasms." An agnostic, and an anti-clerical, he was also to remark: "If you ever go back into religion you will not have been worth the upbringing."

Though there is no evidence that Sylvia was his favourite child he had particularly good relations with her, and to amuse her would often as she told me, sing the song from Shakespeare's *Two Gentlemen of Verona,* "Who Is Sylvia, What Is She?". Punning on the Latin meaning of her name (*silva,* a wood), he would also on occasion call her "Miss Woody Way".[5]

Sylvia's ideas and aspirations were in fact greatly influenced by those of her father whom she was later to speak of as "a standard-bearer of every forlorn hope, every unpopular cause then conceived for the uplifting of oppressed and suffering humanity".

Sylvia was also influenced, though to a lesser extent, and not so clearly, by

Emmeline
Pankhurst, 1906.

her mother Emmeline whom she spoke of with love, though this did not
prevent her from being at times critical of what she considered her mother's
foibles. Though overshadowed by her husband, who was so much her senior,
she was endowed with tenacity and many leadership qualities which were to
become apparent after his death.

Emmeline's father, Robert Goulden, had been a master cotton spinner and
bleacher at Salford. His mother Mary, as Sylvia liked to recall, had been at the
great meeting demanding the extension of the parliamentary franchise, which
was held at St. Peter's Fields, Manchester, in 1819, and was later known on
account of its suppression by the cavalry as the "Massacre of Peterloo". Her
husband was taken by a press gang to serve in the British navy in distant parts
and returned only many years later. Mary Goulden was later, in the "hungry
forties", a member of Richard Cobden's Anti-Corn Law League.

Her son, Robert, Emmeline's father, was an ardent Liberal and a passionate supporter of the North – the anti-slavery side – in the American Civil War. He was very keen on the education of his children, and took his first-born, Emmeline, and later another daughter, Mary, to Paris where he often travelled on business. At the age of thirteen Emmeline was thus placed in the École Normale in the Avenue de Neuilly where she developed a life-long friendship with Noémie Rochefort, the daughter of one of the leaders of the Paris Commune which had been established in 1871 at the close of the Franco-Prussian War, and who was then in exile. Emmeline, who became a passionate Francophile and admirer of Joan of Arc, was soon imbued with French revolutionary ideas, and was proud to discover that she had been born on the anniversary of the fall, on July 14, 1789, of the Bastille, a prison which to her and many of her generation was the ultimate symbol of human despotism.*
In 1885, when Sylvia was three years of age, her father Dr. Pankhurst stood unsuccessfully as a Radical parliamentary candidate for Rotherhithe. His Conservative opponent, Colonel Hamilton, speaking as a "gentleman", attacked him as a "slum politician" who spoke at street corners in the working-class area, among them the notorious Salisbury Street, where he for his part would be "ashamed to be seen".

Not long afterwards the Pankhurst family moved to London where Emmeline, influenced by the ideas of the aesthetic socialist poet William Morris, established a shop, Emerson and Company, at 165 Hampstead Road with the idea of selling artistic objects with which housewives could beautify their homes. The family lived above the shop.

Among the visitors who came there was Alice Brisbane, the American disciple of the French utopian socialist Charles Fourier, and a friend of Sylvia's aunt, Mary Goulden, who, like her sister, had studied in Paris. Sylvia attended Alice's wedding where she met the bride's father who struck her as a gentle old man with fine features. He was, moreover, a remarkable person, for at the age of twenty he had come to Europe to discover "the collective work of man on this earth", and had met many of the European thinkers of his day, among them Karl Marx. Of the latter he observed that, though lacking the genius to advocate "any integral scientific organisation of industry", he had seen "the fundamental weakness of our whole economic system". When Brisbane heard

---

* My mother was also greatly influenced by such ideas. It is significant that on becoming a Suffragette she was to design red Phrygian caps of liberty inspired by those in the French Revolution, and for one women's demonstration devised exact replicas of the banners which had been carried at the St. Peter's Fields franchise meeting in Manchester.

the youthful socialist uttering his first words of protest he had "little imagined" that his theories would later "agitate the world".

Sylvia's governess meanwhile had begun reading to her from the novels of Dickens, Thackeray, Scott and George Eliot. Dickens in particular made a deep impression on her. His writings caused her to have horrible dreams and sleepless nights, perhaps because they gave reality to her father's observations about the people and the poor. Recalling that the miseries of Oliver Twist and other exploited children bit deep into her little heart, she was later to observe, in 1938, that she could no longer read such books, as there was "too much suffering in the actual world". She nonetheless recognised that such writings had bred in her "a great pity for poverty, and a longing, profound and constant, for a Golden Age when plenty and joy should be the gift of all". She could not help wondering what citizens would be produced by Mickey Mouse, Tiger Tim and such-like children's literature of later times.[6] I, her son, was allowed to read such literature, and did so with some amusement, but was never given toy pistols or other juvenile war *matériel*.

The first signs of Sylvia's artistic spirit became apparent at an early age. Her "craving for beauty", as she afterwards wrote, was at the time "insatiable", and she was already attempting to draw at the age of six. One incident which occurred during her infancy left an indelible memory. Her baby brother Frank accidentally destroyed some of her childish "work". Half a century later she recalled:

> Even today a remorseful memory from the days of six years old goads me for a blow never dealt on a little bare buttock crawling before me. Its owner had torn and crumpled some drawing of mine, whilst I dwelt still in the sacred hopefulness of its creation, before the torrential misery of failure to achieve the inner vision had scourged me. High-hearted and engrossed, a pang convulsed me for that destruction. I intended an indignant blow at the departing mischievous one. Yet my hand failed of its purpose, compunction filled my being. The tears welled. The blow became a caress; gently I touched the soft flesh without hurt to the little brother. He crawled on heedless.[7]

The wound of the blow she had thought to deal him nevertheless remained in her heart, and she wept with her head resting on the nursery sewing machine until her eyes saw with surprise a pool of tears.

Not long afterwards, Frank, aged four, was struck down by diphtheria, thought to be due to faulty drains. Her father in his sadness told Sylvia and her sister that they must "never forget Frank". Sylvia, then six years old, cried for him often, though always in secret. Then, she recalls, she tried to draw him "just as he was, but the figure I made on the paper was very ugly, yet I gave it to Father. He encouraged me kindly, saying that he could see Frank in my drawing very clearly." Calmed by his words she "felt an inexpressible throb of gratitude and sympathy; his understanding tenderness seemed like sunshine on my grief-frozen spirit."[8]

After their bereavement the Pankhurst family fled from the house of pestilence. They moved to a large house, 8 Russell Square – at the corner of Barnard Street, now part of the Russell Hotel. The house was decorated by Emmeline in brilliant hues, and on their arrival they found Sylvia's aunt, Mary Goulden, up a ladder painting a drawing-room frieze of irises. The sight of such decorative activity doubtless also conditioned Sylvia's subsequent artistic endeavours.

It was in the Russell Square house that Mrs. Pankhurst gave birth to her fifth child, Henry Francis, better known as Harry, in July 1889. To his mother the expected infant was "Frank coming again". To Sylvia, when he arrived, he was "the loveliest child that ever was". To hold him was "joy"; to be allowed on some rare occasions, to share her bed with him, was "rapture". She lay awake, with arms about him, holding her breath lest he might wake.[9] Her relations with Frank were indeed to be particularly warm throughout his life, far closer than with either of her sisters.

The Russell Square house was a hive of political activity. Visitors included politicians and political thinkers of many "advanced" hues: Socialists, Anarchists, Radicals, Republicans, Nationalists, suffragists, free thinkers, agnostics, atheists and humanitarians of all kinds. Among them were the Italian Anarchist Malatesta, the Russian refugees Kropotkin, Stepniak, and Nicholas Tchaykovsky, Henri Rochefort (whose daughter was still in close contact with young Mrs. Pankhurst), the American apostle of Negro freedom William Lloyd Garrison, and Dadabhai Naoroji, the first Indian member of the British House of Commons. Other callers included William Morris, Herbert Borrows – the enthusiastic organiser of the matchgirls' strike of 1888 – and the feminist Annie Besant. Perhaps the person who most struck the youthful Sylvia was, however, the French woman Louise Michel who had been active in the Paris Commune almost a generation earlier. The "Petrouleuse" as her enemies called her was by then a tiny old woman in a brown cloak, intensely lean, with gleaming eyes and a swarthy skin which made Sylvia think of the twisted seams in the bark of an ancient chestnut tree. She had a beaming eye for children, so much so, the aspiring young artist says, that:

I regarded her with admiration as a tremendous heroine. She seemed to belong to the magical world of imagination, not the commonplace life of every day. Sometimes I fancied her wandering in strange old forests amid the fantastic beings of fairy-tales; at others I saw her in the stress of battle, her slight figure leaping forward in the darkness, lit by a glare of conflagration, her bare arm uplifted with a torch, a scarlet Phrygian cap upon her raven hair, wide-mouthed with a shout of defiance, her lips drawn back from gleaming teeth, her black eyes sparkling with fierce joy.[10]

This was, however, a time when people were looking less to the past than to the future. The Fabian Society had been founded in 1883–4, and the Pankhurst circle was reading the *Fabian Essays*, the short-lived Socialist magazine *Today*, which contained articles by George Bernard Shaw, as well as Kropotkin's *Fields, Factories and Workshops*, Edward Bellamy's *Looking Backward*, and Robert Blatchford's *Merrie England*. The question of the status of women was likewise coming increasingly to the fore. In 1891, a judge had decided in the famous Jackson case that a husband was not entitled to kidnap and imprison his wife, and Sylvia as a nine-year-old heard the song then popular in Christmas pantomimes, "Ho! ho! the Jackson case".

She and her sisters took a keen interest in the many and varied political meetings which their parents were constantly arranging in the house. The children helped to arrange chairs, gave out leaflets, and passed round pretty little brocade bags for collections. Sylvia, because of her evident skill at drawing, was ever in demand to print notices, in big uncertain letters, one of the most common being "To the Tea Room", for there were always refreshments, with strawberries whenever in season picked in the garden.

When not so engaged she was busy on her own youthful projects which included drawing, writing, copying the embroidery on a Japanese screen – or watching insects or worms in the garden and in the nearby Russell Square where she and her sisters often played. Once she saw a toad there, and having previously known this reptile only from pictures, was full of excitement. She recalled Shakespeare's phrase in *As You Like It*: "The toad, ugly and venomous, wears yet a precious jewel in his head." Though aware that there was in reality no jewel she searched for it carefully, and "thought with pleasure that its eyes were more lovely than precious stones". She took it in her hands, and looked with wonder at its short, weak legs and tiny, clutching "fingers". She imagined that it had become a little baby, and that they were floating together over the clouds.

She spent innumerable hours in the wooded square, the pale-blue larkspur of which seemed lovelier than anything on earth, and in the garden behind the house. This was a tiny patch of ground, without any flowers, enclosed by a bleak high wall; but there she would sit imagining adventures, as she poetically recalls:

> The wall would fade away, vistas of trees and flowers would take its place; a lake with swans and waterlilies; a river flowing through meadows, and fringed with yellow irises. Birds sang; lambs floundered upon the grass; a lovely woman in white robes came smiling towards me, surrounded by dancing children. I flew away on the back of a great bird, I soared above the clouds, I crossed the seas. I descended to yellow sands, where groves of palms and flowering trees came near to the water's edge, and barges lay moored, laden with bright fruits, gorgeous silks, wrought silver and gold and precious stones, all the richest and loveliest things my child mind could conceive.[11]

She was interested in a childish, yet romantic and artistic way in the botany of the garden, as the thought of growth seemed "magical":

> The seed bursting its sheath, and putting forth its first pale shoot, caused a thrill of rapture. The sight of the fallen leaves was always sad; yet as I stood looking with my eyes fixed upon them, would come the thought of life stirring under the leaves; and presently I would see trees arising from them; trees such as never were, forever changing, growing from the dear, familiar trees one knew and loved, to marvellous creations, bearing wonderful, unknown fruits, with squirrels, lizards, birds of every hue, playing in their branches, which, reaching higher and higher into the skies, supported fair castles in the air. The goal of those dreams was always one cherished climax; a beautiful country house surrounded by daisied lawns, with woods and fields beyond. Peacocks displayed their gorgeous tails upon the terraces, dappled fawns fed, confident, from the hand, pigeons cooed in the woods, little green love-birds perched in the carpets on the wall. Everything of beauty and desire I saw or read of, found a place in that pleasant scheme.

This "house of blessing" was soon surrounded by many others; for whoever so desired would be free to live there, and there "the poor and sad would find plenty and joy".

On other days she and her sisters emulated the grown-ups by playing at dressmaking. They cut and stitched clothes for their dolls, but soon put them away, and took no further interest in them for many months.

Another pastime, at night when the girls went to bed, was to tell each other what they could see in the dark with their faces on the pillow. "Wonderful processions and pageants passed by lovelier than one could tell. The shyness and restraint of the day would vanish, and one could speak with a freedom unknown at other times."[12]

One day, having dreamt that a witch had transformed her and her sisters into three grey cats and transported them to a desert island, she wrote the story as a play. She made the scenery with the help of her uncle, Robert Goulden, a screen painter by profession, who had come down to spend Christmas in London. He made the scenery, including the wings, with stout brown paper. It was all "magnificently professional" in Sylvia's eyes, though she could not help hoping for something still more wondrous, more in keeping with the beautiful imagery of her dreams. On another occasion she and her sisters dramatised Heinrich Hoffman's cautionary tale *Harriette and the Matches*, Sylvia being Harriette, and Christabel and Adela the cats.[13]

Sylvia and her sisters, unlike the more passive youngsters of the present television age, were brought up to create their own pastimes. Besides play-acting they published a manuscript weekly (later monthly) newspaper for circulation among the family. It was called *The Home News* and bore a sub-title, chosen by her father, *and Universal Mirror*. The Doctor contributed serious articles on social and political subjects, while Sylvia drew the illustrations – and wrote a series of articles entitled "Walks in London", describing visits to the House of Commons, the British Museum, the National Gallery, the Tower of London and other places.[14] Before long she and her sisters were reporting on the women's suffrage meetings they were attending.[15]

Sylvia, Christabel and Adela went on many walks all over London which, she later recalled, was then "more picturesque to a child" than subsequently:

> ... there were carriages with beautiful horses, and the delightful hansom cabs wherein it was such a joy to ride, such an excitement, one seemed to speed like the wind. Punch and Judy was much more often seen, more prosperous, richer in colour, more patronised. Then there were Scotsmen in their kilts who played bag-pipes, the muffin man, always heard on Sundays, and women selling lavender with their pretty song. The tradesmen were surely more intimate and more friendly; the grocer giving me biscuits because I resembled, he said, the little girl on the show-card; the butcher sending home sweetbreads as a present to 'the three young ladies', meaning we three, the eldest of whom was ten; and the often repeated question in the shops to our diminutive Welsh nurse: 'Are they all yours?' when she was out with all four of us, which pleased her immensely. How proud she was of us, dear Susannah!

Once when they were in sight of Queen Victoria, Susannah claimed that Her Majesty had gazed on young Harry with special interest, but Sylvia, as a Republican, refused to experience any exaltation at this.[16]

The Pankhurst girls were under the care at this time of a governess, Cecile

Left to right: Sylvia, Adela, Christabel Pankhurst, *c.* 1890.

Sowerby, an artist whom Aunt Mary had known in Paris. Miss Sowerby gave them no formal lessons, but read to them and took them to museums, galleries and other places of interest. Much of the children's time was spent in the British Museum where Sylvia's greatest enthusiasm was for the Egyptian section, the massive shapes and gorgeous colours of which left "a deep and permanent fascination" on her, while the knowledge that those vivacious scenes and pigments were "older than history" lent an added thrill. The mummy cases, with their pictured life stories, woke in her inmost thoughts the longing to solve the mysteries of life and death. She became eager to understand the construction of the human frame, and begged to see a skeleton. Miss Sowerby would have taken them to a medical museum for this purpose, but only adults were allowed admission. Dr. Pankhurst therefore brought home a cardboard anatomical man, the muscular system, vital organs and skeleton of which were revealed by turning back successive layers of the card.[17]

Princess Toutebelle and the yellow dwarf, from Walter Crane's shilling toy book *The Yellow Dwarf*, London, 1874.

Aladdin approached by his pretended uncle, from Walter Crane's shilling toy book *Aladdin; or The Wonderful Lamp*, London, 1874.

Sylvia, unlike her sister Christabel who began reading at an incredibly early age, did not read much until relatively late, for she suffered from poor eyesight, and her parents feared to make it worse. However, when she was nearly eight years of age she was unhappy because her nurse stumbled when reading an English translation of Jules Verne's *De la terre à la lune,* and, taking the book from her hands, decided that she would henceforth read herself.[18]

The Doctor was always buying books for his children, among them Routledge's shilling Toy Books which were illustrated by the Socialist artist Walter Crane, a disciple of William Morris, from which they sang old English songs. Sylvia was particularly struck by Crane's Socialist cartoons, and especially his notable drawing "Triumph of Labour" designed to commemorate International Labour Day, May 1, 1891.*

She was familiar with the drawing "When Adam Delved and Eve Span, who was then the Gentleman?" with which William Morris had illustrated his *Dream of John Ball* as well as with Morris' Kelmscott books and many of his

---

* This painting likewise impressed one of the principal authorities on Crane, P.G.Konody, who observed that in it the artist rose to "real greatness. I know of but few black-and-white drawings that are worthy to be placed by its side." P.G.Konody, *The Art of Walter Crane* (London 1902), p. 82.

WHEN ADAM DELVED
AND EVE SPAN·
WHO WAS THEN THE
GENTLEMAN

Left: "When Adam delved and Eve span, who was then the gentleman", from William Morris' *A Dream of John Ball*, London, 1888.

Below: "Triumph of Labour", a drawing designed by Walter Crane to commemorate International Labour Day, May 1, 1891.

fabrics. The works of William Morris and Walter Crane made a deep impression on her, and aroused in her the longing to be a decorative painter and draughtsman in the service of great movements for social betterment. "I would", she was later to write, "portray the world that is to be when poverty is no more. I would decorate halls where people would foregather in the movement to win the new world, and make banners for meetings and processions." Having been with her parents to meetings of the Social Democratic Federation in dingy rooms in back streets, and to drab and dreary demonstrations in Hyde Park, she wanted to make them more beautiful. Such were the ambitions of her youth.[19]

It was in fact not long before she was devoting many hours a day to drawing with pencils and painting with watercolours. She was "constantly drawing things – not things seen, always things imagined". She was, however, intensely shy of showing anyone her work. Her sketchbooks were in consequence most carefully hidden, generally under the furniture, for, she says, "I was too keenly conscious of my failure to render adequately my visions, to endure without pain the inspection of my efforts by the relatively indifferent gaze of other eyes. Only when the original conceptions had been thrust, by a succession of others, into the background of my mind, and thus their sacredness was dimmed, would a drawing-book be carelessly left about, and so get picked up and examined by other people."[20]

Aunt Mary, who enjoyed Sylvia's childhood trust, also on occasion persuaded her to let her see her youthful works, and then to show them to the Doctor.

The quest for knowledge was soon a favourite subject of Sylvia's drawings: "Half-nude figures bearing loads in the rocky mountains, buildings with rude stone boulders, bearing lamps through the darkness, their unshod feet treading the rude and jagged stones; old scholars poring over great tomes and surrounded by scales and crucibles."[21]

Her artistic and political ideas were sharpened when Harriet Stanton Blatch, an active member of the Women's Franchise League, took her and Christabel to stay with her own daughter, Norah, at her home in Basingstoke. This visit made a deep impression on my mother, who throughout her life was perhaps always happier in a rural than an urban environment. "What a joy," she exclaimed, "that country was to me, a town-bred child who had rarely been beyond the suburbs! The canal, with its waterlilies and irises, and the fields of scarlet poppies, seemed like the realisation of a dream."[22] The countryside seemed to her indeed a "children's land". On returning to London she wept "at the sight of the grey streets, with beggars, and piteous ragged children, many of whom, even in the winter, were without shoes to protect their poor little muddy feet"[23] – an all too common sight in the England of those days.

⁂ 2 School; the Independent Labour Party; Keir Hardie; the Manchester School of Art

IN THE WINTER of 1892–3 the five-year lease of the Pankhursts' house in Russell Square came to an end. The family moved to Southport, a Mersey watering place within easy reach of Manchester in and around which the Doctor practised as a lawyer. It was decided that Christabel and Sylvia, then twelve and ten years old respectively, should be sent to the local high school for girls. Their younger sister, Adela, aged seven, though held by Mrs. Pankhurst to be too young, insisted on attending too.

Sylvia studied with zest, and increasing interest. One day her teacher drew on the blackboard a picture of the kind of hut in which the ancient Britons lived. "You can all try to draw that," she said, "but I don't think any of you could draw an ancient Briton." Sylvia, responding to the challenge, at once said that she thought she could, and the teacher asked her to try. The young artist went eagerly to the board, and quickly sketched a figure which won warm praise both from the mistress and the class. Teacher said it could remain up for a week, and the principal, Mr. Ross, and his wife, came in to see it, and offered words of encouragement.[1]

The Pankhursts, however, moved that summer to Disley in rural Cheshire, some sixteen miles from Manchester, and took rooms in a farmhouse. The children accordingly left the school at Southport after only one term, and were obliged to continue their education with the governess of two girls of the village. Sylvia, whose artistic temperament often caused her to withdraw from the company of her sisters, spent much of the time in the fields, painting landscapes and scribbling poetry in the company only of her fox-terrier, Vic.

In the autumn her parents returned to Manchester the smoke of which Sylvia detested, for it blackened the masonry and bleached the skin of its citizens. The family made its home at 4 Buckingham Crescent, Victoria Park. It was arranged for the children to go to Manchester High School, the discipline and routine of which seemed oppressive after the free life to which they had been accustomed.

Sylvia hated the school though she enjoyed some of the lessons. She made no friends among her fellow pupils, some of whom hated her for not attending scripture classes – her parents being agnostics – while others disliked her for espousing the cause of the "scholarship students" who on account of their humble origins and poor clothes were shunned by the fee-paying pupils. She nevertheless won the admiration of many on account of her drawings. Her teacher, evidently struck by her ability, asked if she might take modelling and drawing with the girls of the upper school, but the headmistress, Miss Elizabeth Day, refused to agree to this.

Sylvia was soon bored by what she considered the excessive time devoted to mathematics, French verbs and the repetition of historical and geographical facts, and by the vast amount of homework expected of her. She nevertheless seized upon any and every excuse to introduce drawing into her work, and spent the greater part of every evening on such sketches, though this obliged her to sit up late to finish her hateful arithmetic. The latter she accepted without demur, she and her sisters being indeed such quiet and well-behaved children that great astonishment was expressed by the teachers who had known them when they soon afterwards emerged to militancy in the suffragette movement.[2]

A cartoon by an unknown artist of the early 1880s, depicting Keir Hardie carrying the unemployed into the House of Commons. The Socialist MP had just then introduced a motion deploring the fact that the government's policy, as laid down in the Queen's speech, made no provision of aid to the unemployed.
PHOTO: THE LABOUR PARTY

Though capable of energetic action and forthright speaking on public issues my mother was in fact throughout her life gentle and well-mannered; she invariably spoke quietly if often with authority and a sense of conviction.

By now in her early 'teens Sylvia would go on Sundays with her father, who had joined the Independent Labour party, the ILP as it was generally called, at its inception in 1893, to Ancoats, Gorton, Hulme and other working-class districts. There, standing on a chair or box, he would speak to the people about their misery and the way to alleviate it. Sylvia was perhaps the most earnest member of his audience, but she was as ever saddened by the ugliness of the dwellings in which the people of the area lived – "those endless rows of smoke-begrimed little houses, with never a tree or flower in sight". She recalls:

> Many a time in spring, as I gazed upon them, those two red may trees in our garden at home would rise up in my mind, almost menacing in their beauty; and I would ask myself whether it was just that I should live in Victoria Park, and go well fed and warmly clad, whilst the children of these grey slums were lacking the very necessities of life. The misery of the poor, as I heard my father plead for it, and saw it revealed in the pinched faces of his audiences, awoke in me a maddening sense of impotence; and there were moments when I had an impulse to dash my head against the dreary walls of those squalid streets.[3]

A notable event of this period, and one which she was to remember throughout her life, was her first meeting, as a child of eleven in 1893, with the veteran Scottish Socialist Keir Hardie. He was the founder of the ILP whose newspaper, the *Labour Leader,* had made its appearance as a weekly in the previous March, and was already a welcome messenger to the entire Pankhurst family. The journal was expressive of its unassuming editor who conversed in homely strain to his readers. "That poor devil, Bernard Shaw, is in trouble again: he has fallen downstairs and broken his leg!" was a characteristic utterance in the personal vein which relieved the tedium of political pronouncements so common in other Socialist circles.

Describing her first encounter with this much respected, almost legendary figure, whose portrait she was later twice to attempt, she recalls:

> To me he was a tremendous hero, before all others the champion of the workers, who had arisen from themselves to lead them to the promised land when "Man to Man, the world o'er shall brothers be for a' that". I had seen the cartoon of him carrying the unemployed on his back into the House of Commons. I had heard my father, with a tremble of enthusiasm in his voice, praising the brave stand Keir Hardie had made in Parliament. I hurried home from school that day, knowing that he had already arrived. Seeing the library door ajar, I hastened upstairs to the

angle where one could see who was sitting in the big armchair by the fire. There he was; his majestic head surrounded by ample curls going grey and shining with glints of silver and golden brown; his great forehead deeply lined; his eyes, two deep wells of kindness, like mountain pools with the sunlight distilled they always seemed to me. Friendship radiated from him. Kneeling on the stairs to watch him I felt that I could have rushed into his arms; instead it was not long before the children in the houses where he stayed had climbed to his knees. He had at once the appearance of great age and great youth. Like a sturdy oak, with its huge trunk seamed and gnarled, and its garlands of summer leaves, he seemed to carry with him the spirit of nature in the great open spaces.[4]

Sylvia, though still too young to join the ILP – she could not do so until her sixteenth birthday – fully identified herself with the nascent Socialist party. When her father stood as its parliamentary candidate for Gorton in 1895 she and her sister Christabel went daily with their mother to join in the canvassing. Many people, she found, had something kind to say about the Doctor, and not a few of them told her they would vote for him next time, because for the present he had no chance of being elected. The vote, she sadly realised, seemed to many a kind of game, in which it was important to be on the winning side. These were in fact difficult times for the Socialists, and before Gorton polled it was announced that Keir Hardie had been defeated at West Ham.

Political activity nonetheless continued, and there was much excitement in the Pankhurst family, as well as in Manchester ILP circles generally, when in the summer of 1896 members of the party were imprisoned for speaking in the Boggart Hole Clough, an open space acquired by the city council for public use. Mrs. Pankhurst was one of a number of speakers who continued to hold meetings there in defiance of the authorities, and Sylvia had her name written down by a policeman for helping to take a collection.

Despite increasing interest and involvement in ILP activities in Manchester she continued to draw and read. When her schooling came to an end she spent much of her time with her drawing materials, supremely content. John Ruskin and Richard Jefferies were the writers who especially attracted her in this period.

Early in the summer of 1898 she was allowed, to her great delight, to take lessons with Elias Bancroft, a well-known Manchester artist of the time, who lived at the other end of Buckingham Crescent. Writing of her studies with him she says:

Whatman's drawing paper, stamps and rubbers of squeezed bread, came to my knowledge as a revelation. I felt a sense of power in seeing the rounded shapes stand forth from my blank paper, and the rich chiaroscuro which charcoal could produce. I revelled in still life groups, and at home, arranging jars, bowls and foliage to my own fancy, attempted to reproduce them in watercolours.[5]

She drew each day for as many hours as she could, completely absorbed and fascinated by the new-found methods. Though none of her work of this period remains it is evident that she had advanced far since the old days in Russell Square when she attempted to draw only from imagination.

Later that summer when Sylvia was sixteen her father – and hero – died, and her entire world crashed about her. His death left the family at once without its mentor and its bread-winner.* Dr. Pankhurst's electioneering had moreover created many debts, and his widow, insistent on paying creditors to the full, had no alternative but to sell much of their property. Charles Rowley, an ardent Pre-Raphaelite who ran the Ancoats Brotherhood, and sought to introduce to the workers of Manchester the best examples of music, art and science, came to advise as to the value of the pictures belonging to Dr. Pankhurst, and how they could best be disposed of. On that occasion he saw some of Sylvia's drawings, and declared that she was "more promising than the pictures". Her still life groups were accordingly despatched to the Manchester School of Art, and to her great joy, it was not long before she was awarded a free studentship there.

Her ensuing time at the art school was one of immense satisfaction. "In spite of our grief and my nervous depression, when absorbed in the work", she observed, "I knew the greatest happiness. Students and teachers all were kind, especially that generous enthusiast, Henry Cadness, who presided over the design school."

In her first year at the school she was however so tortured by neuralgia in her head and arms that she was often obliged to stay at home. In her weak state, standing to draw and model led to a slight but obstinate internal weakness, and she was so tormented by chilblains that she had to go out of the hot life room to gain relief by pouring on her feet the methylated spirits they used for fixing the drawings.

During her stay at the school Owen's College, Manchester, celebrated its golden jubilee and in this connection the Whitworth Hall was opened on

---

* Mrs. Pankhurst was later appointed a registrar of births and deaths, a post which assured her a modest income, and, being assisted by an assistant registrar, sufficient time to devote herself to social and political work.

March 12, 1902, by the Prince of Wales, later King George V. An illuminated address of welcome was prepared by the principal, teachers and some of the more promising students of the art school, each being allotted a page to design and illuminate. Sylvia was one of those so honoured. She applied herself, "for Art's sake", to make the work – which cannot unfortunately be traced – as beautiful as she could. Nevertheless as a Republican she took part no less eagerly in Socialist propaganda organised in connection with the royal visit by the local ILP of which she was by then a member.

She and her Socialist comrades spent the day selling two of Keir Hardie's publications, an "Open Letter to the King", and a pamphlet on unemployment. She found the public largely hostile, on which account most of the other sellers gave up. She persevered, however, and by the end of the day had broken the record by selling two pounds' worth of literature.[6]

Her studies at the Manchester School of Art coincided with the Boer War, which was strongly opposed by many Radicals, her mother and sisters included. When Adela expressed the family's anti-imperialist views at her own school, she was struck in the face by a book, thrown at her across the class-room in the presence of a teacher who watched the incident without intervening. Tempers at the School of Art likewise ran high. On one occasion Sylvia's artistic hero Walter Crane, a former director of design at the school, came to lecture on ornament. He illustrated his talk by drawing Britannia's trident, and interpolated, "Let her be as careful to respect the liberties of others as she is in safeguarding her own!" Sylvia wrote a report of the lecture for the school's manuscript magazine, in which she referred to Crane's remark, whereupon one of the jingoistic students, Cecily Fox Smith, the subsequent author of books on seafaring and London inns, dashed off to the editor to demand the suppression of the report, and declared that she would follow Miss Pankhurst home and break the windows of her house.

During her first year at the art school she had been so often away on account of illness that she felt unjustified in holding a free scholarship, the more so as she wished to help her mother and elder sister in another shop, again called Emerson and Company, that they were then trying to run at 40 and 42 King Street, Manchester. She therefore proposed that for the second year she should study only part-time as a paying student which would be relatively inexpensive. She soon found, however, that she had nothing to do at the shop except to write window tickets. Despite her limited attendance at the school at the end of the school year, in 1901, she was named the best woman student of the year, and was awarded the Lady Whitworth Scholarship of thirty pounds and free tuition. She therefore resumed full-time attendance at the school.

In the following year, 1902, she won the National Silver Medal for mosaic designs, the Primrose Medal, and, of even greater interest, the Proctor Travelling Studentship – the highest prize open to students at her school – a vacation scholarship enabling its holder to make a short visit abroad. Students were entirely free to select where they would like to go. Doubtless influenced by the fact that many British artists, Walter Crane included, had drawn so much of their inspiration from residence in Italy, she chose Venice to study mosaics, and Florence for its frescoes.

ᶿᶿᶿ 3 Venice; Pankhurst Hall, Salford; the Founding of the WSPU

SYLVIA's travelling scholarship was a source of great joy to Mrs. Pankhurst who decided to go with her daughter as far as Geneva to stay with her old schoolfriend Noémie Rochefort, who had by then married the Swiss artist Auguste Frédéric Dufaux (their two sons Henri and Armand were notable pioneers of aviation). Mother and daughter travelled by way of Ostend to Bruges with which city Sylvia was so charmed that she was loth to leave it. They then made their way to Brussels where she lost her heart to the ornate architectural riches of the Hôtel de Ville. In the train to Switzerland her thoughts were full of the mellow glories of Belgian art, the tranquil radiance of the Belgian countryside and the tuneful chiming old belfry at Bruges. As the journey proceeded the country became increasingly mountainous and many weary hours later she was thrilled when there was a sudden gap in the mountains and she saw through it the waters of Lake Geneva, a far, ethereal blue, ineffably soft and clear.

During their stay in Geneva, Monsieur Dufaux spent the mornings painting a portrait of Mrs. Pankhurst, whom he made to appear young and round faced. Sylvia drew her mother too, in pencil, but she produced an older and very sad woman. (The sketch unfortunately does not seem to have been kept.)

"Elle cherche bien les formes," commented Dufaux. Sylvia was happy to receive the Swiss artist's encouragement, though she testifies that she was by no means satisfied with her work. She was ever a perfectionist, and for that reason many of her drawings, poems and other literary works never saw the light of day. The afternoons were largely spent rowing on the lake, the shining loveliness of which caused her once more to wish to call a halt to her journey to Italy.

When the time to depart approached Madame Dufaux persuaded Mrs. Pankhurst that they should accompany Sylvia as far as Venice. The young artist was stunned by the grandeur of the mountain views seen from the train, and entranced by the picturesque glimpses of peasant life: women labouring in the fields, cottages with maize and tunny fish drying on the walls, bare-footed children happily at play. Eventually came the hour-long ride across the great railway bridge to Venice. Seeing the city for the first time in the soft, iridescent gold of the setting sun, she found it a wonderful contrast to the grime of urban England, and described it as:

> A wondrous city of fairest carving, reflected in gleaming waters swirled to new patterning by every passing gondola. Venice in the brief, violet twilight; Venice in the mournful loveliness of pale marble palaces, rising in the velvet darkness of the night; the promised land of my sad young heart, craving for beauty, fleeing from the sorrowful ugliness of factory-ridden Lancashire, and the dull, aching poverty of its slums; Venice, O city of dreaming magic![1]

She and her mother were guided through this beautiful city by Madame Dufaux. The latter was but a modest aide for she had no knowledge of languages. She had only one oft-repeated English phrase, "Shudder-door!" and a single Italian word, "Avanti", which she thought meant "Go away". She and Mrs. Pankhurst both advised Sylvia to remember the latter word in case anyone molested her, but the supposed talisman seemed only of limited efficacy, for whenever Madame Dufaux used it the crowd of urchins begging for money failed to disappear; indeed the more she shouted "Avanti!" the closer they approached her until she had no option but to throw them a handful of small coins.[2]

Madame Dufaux and Mrs. Pankhurst left Venice as planned at the end of the week, and Sylvia took up her abode with a middle-aged English woman who had gone to Italy on a scholarship for historical research from Victoria University, Manchester. She lived in a flat in one of the smaller of the old marble palaces, the residence in the Calle dell' Arco, San Antonino, of Countess Sophie Bertelli Algarotti, a Polish widow of an Italian count. Repelled by the city's summer heat Madame Sophie, as she was generally called, had retired to her native Poland, leaving her tenant the right to take paying guests. There in an early nineteenth-century salon upholstered with yellow satin, its walls draped with yellow brocade and covered with old-fashioned pictures, and gilded chairs, the young artist, full of anguish, and her eyes streaming with tears, bade a sad farewell to her mother.

In the weeks which followed she nevertheless found solace in her work, and soon revelled in the quietness of her surroundings, so full of grace and beauty. She no longer saw any newspapers, and for reading matter devoted herself only to the poets. Determined to make use of every available minute she rose each morning at five and went out to paint until eight. Then, after breakfast, she would proceed to St. Mark's Cathedral to copy the famous mosaics, to San Giorgio degli Schiavoni to study the Carpaccios, or to one or other church, or to the Accademia for some such artistic purpose. In the afternoon she would go to the Rialto to paint its crowds, to the Cà d'Oro, or to some gaily furnished shop or stall to depict its colourful vendors. At the end of the day she tried to paint on her balcony by moonlight, but was obliged to stop as her hands trembled with fatigue.

When people gathered to watch her working she would take out her sketchbook and ask them to allow her to paint their portraits. They invariably agreed, and she would work eagerly and in haste amidst admiring shouts of "Brava ! Brava !" as the picture emerged. On one occasion, early in her stay, the children crowded so closely around that she felt faint from the heat. Her easel was almost knocked over, and her paint-box almost trampled on. Remembering Madame Dufaux's magic word she cried out "Avanti ! Avanti !", but the youngsters merely came closer, laughing and shouting more loudly. Eventually two men broke through the crowd, helped her to gather up her property, and put her on her way home. She thus learnt the true meaning of the word "Avanti !".

This was her only disturbing incident in Venice, for usually one or two members of the crowd would constitute themselves the guardians of law and order, and would control the throng for her. While in the streets her work would be discussed in a lively manner; sometimes the young girls commented that she was "brutta", or plain, while the older women answered, "Si si, ma simpatica."

At the end of the summer Sylvia joined the Accademia delle Belle Arti, where she wanted to study in the life class under an artist called Tito. He seems to have been embarrassed at the idea of having a woman participating with the men students in the drawing of nudes, for on the first day he sent her to the antique room where no one else was working. Realising that she would never enter the life class if she waited there, the next day she made her way into the class by herself. "So you are here !" he remarked when he saw her. Thenceforth he treated her just like any other student. The men students were shy in her presence, but behaved politely. Knowing no other language but Italian, they nevertheless kept their distance. She let them believe she did not understand Italian, though she could soon follow everything they said. She did this because she feared that if they knew she was listening to them her presence

32

No. 1: Untitled. St. Theodora, copied from a mosaic in St. Mark's Cathedral, Venice.

No. 2: Untitled. The prophet Micah copied from mosaics in St. Mark's Cathedral, Venice.

would be the more embarrassing. As it was they soon spoke among each other as if she was not present. Much of the talk was on marriage. Most of them rejected it in favour of celibacy for artists of their age, but one advocated the opposite view, and several would not commit themselves. Throughout her stay in the Accademia, Sylvia, as she later recalled, was "a shy girl who did not speak." She was, however, happy among these Italian art students, and "glad", she said, of "their clean thoughts and enthusiasm for their art."[3]

She also attended the Accademia delle Belle Arti's landscape class, in this case with several other women students. Her teacher Ciardi gave her much encouragement, and having left behind the work she did with him, to her surprise she later received a diploma.

Among her extant paintings almost a dozen seem to have been produced in this period. (Complete certainty is not possible for scarcely any of her artistic work is dated, and, as we shall see, she was to return to Venice in 1906, though only for about a week, so that a few, but not many, of those here

No. 3: Untitled. The Angel at the Tomb of Christ with the Three Maries, copied from the mosaic in St. Mark's Cathedral, Venice.

mentioned may in fact date from the later visit.)

Of the studies she made of Italian art – most if not all during her first stay in the city – there exists a copy of the head and shoulders of the mosaic of St. Theodora from St. Mark's cathedral. The watercolour (No. 1) is executed in great detail, with touches of Prussian blue ink. This fine mosaic portrait with remarkably expressive facial moulding in different shades and stylised hair evidently caught her imagination. The picture was a great favourite of hers, and, with a copy of the mosaic of the prophet Micah, also from St. Mark's, hung prominently in later years in her house in Woodford Green, and subsequently in her study in Addis Ababa (in which, after her death, I was later to work). The Prophet Micah was damaged on the journey from England to Ethiopia, and only the face remains (No. 2).

No. 4: Untitled. Study of Carpaccio's *Triumph of St. George* in Venice.

A third watercolour study (No. 3), in coloured ink and gold paint, of the angel at the tomb with the three Maries from the arch between the nave cupola and the central cupola at St. Mark's also seems to date from this period.

Her admiration for Carpaccio is evident from her copy (No. 4) of a detail from *The Triumph of Saint George* in watercolours, heightened with coloured ink.

Three sketches of Venice streets are characteristic of her interest in the common people and their work – an interest, possibly inspired by her father's teaching, which was to dominate her later painting and indeed ultimately to take her entirely outside the field of art. One painting, in watercolours and coloured ink (No. 5), is of an Italian fruit and vegetable seller almost engulfed by her wares, with her scales and prices prominently displayed. Another fruit vendor, this time an old man, is depicted, again in watercolour, under the arches of the Rialto market (No. 6). A third market scene (Plate I), in gouache

No. 5: Untitled. An Italian fruit and vegetable seller surrounded by her wares.

No. 6: *Fruit Seller: Rialto Venice Market.*

and watercolour on brown ochre paper, depicts a stall with a bell tower and arcade in the background.

A charming watercolour with touches of gouache and coloured ink (No. 7) shows the artist's fascination with the beauties of Venice: a little bridge linking two palazzi across a narrow canal. On the steps are two healthy little girls. The southern European foliage overhanging the garden wall, the bright Mediterranean light, and the architectural details of the palazzo occupying most of the background are all carefully observed, and convey the artist's excitement with the city which contrasted so dramatically with the gloomy Lancashire towns she knew in her youth.

Another delightful street scene (Plate III) shows an urchin in a red cap and blue cape looking with bright-eyed curiosity at the artist. In the background a cluster of autumnal trees.

Her most ambitious surviving work of this period is an oil painting (No. 8) of a canal, with a barge laden with sacks in the foreground. It is painted in

Opposite: No. 7: Untitled. A Venetian scene.

Left: No. 8: Untitled. A view of a canal in Venice.

Below: The artist's signature as it appears on most of her early works.

SCHEME·OF DECORATION FOR·THE PANKHURST·HALL

AS·THIS·HALL·BEARS·THE NAME·OF·A·PIONEER·WHOSE· LIFE·WAS·GIVEN·FOR·THE·IDEAL AND·FOR·THE·FUTURE·EMBLEMS OF·THE·FUTURE·AND·THE·IDEAL HAVE·BEEN·CHOSEN·WITH WHICH·TO·DECORATE·IT

THE·ENTRANCE·HALL THE·SYMBOLS·ARE:———THE! PEACOCK'S·FEATHER·LILY·&·ROSE EMBLEMS·OF·BEAUTY·PURITY &·LOVE; WITH·THE·MOTTO:—— ENGLAND·ARISE!·AND·THE THE·NAME·OF·THE·HALL

THE·LARGE·HALL SYMBOLS:— ROSES·CLOVE· APPLE·TREES··KNOWLEDGE DOVES··PEACE,

CORN··PLENTY·, LILIES·· PURITY, HONESTY··HONESTY· BEES··INDUSTRY; SUNFLOWER AND··BUTTERFLIES··HOPE.

THE·PANELS·ILLUSTRATE SHELLEY'S·LINES:— HOPE·WILL·MAKE·THEE·YOUNG, FOR·HOPE·&·YOUTH, ARE·CHILDREN·OF·ONE MOTHER·EVER, LOVE.

SYLVIA·PANKHURST· STUDIO·30·KING·STREET

No. 9: Artistic conception of the decorations for Pankhurst Hall, Salford, 1903.

quiet brown, russets and yellows, possibly in the late afternoon, and was another of the works my mother was most pleased with. It was hung where she could see it easily, in Woodford Green and later in Addis Ababa, where it seemed transformed by the bright Ethiopian sunlight.

Sylvia was so happy in Venice that she abandoned her original idea of proceeding to Florence. She was reinforced in this decision by the entreaties of Madame Sophie who had by then returned to Italy and to whom she had become greatly attached. The Polish woman, whose father, a great patriot, had devoted the family's fortune to the national struggle for independence from Russia, took a kindly interest in the young English art student and went so far as to urge her to remain with her permanently as her friend and daughter who, she insisted, would have no expenses.

Sylvia dallied in Venice after her scholarship expired, but felt duty-bound to return home in the spring of 1903. She was confirmed in this decision by receipt of a letter from her sister Christabel announcing that, following in their father's footsteps, she intended to prepare to matriculate at Victoria University, in order to become a barrister. Sylvia would therefore be needed by her mother, both at home, and in their shop, where her artistic talents were expected to be useful. She accordingly left Venice without more ado.[4]

On returning to Manchester she found that during her absence her mother had hired a studio for her above the shop in King Street, and had promised that her daughter would decorate a hall which the ILP had built in St. James's Road, Hightown, Salford, in memory of Dr. Pankhurst.* The opening date had already been fixed, and the twenty-one-year-old artist had in fact only three weeks to do the work. She at once set to, and prepared the designs which abounded with scrolls, and representations of fruit and flowers. Her artistic conception is apparent from a draft, in her own hand, which is still extant. It declares:

> As this hall bears the name of a pioneer whose life was given for the ideal and for the future, emblems of the future and the ideal have been chosen with which to decorate it.
>
> The Entrance Hall. The symbols are the peacock's feather, lily & rose, emblems of beauty, purity & love; with the motto: "England arise!" and the name of the hall.
>
> The Large Hall. Symbols: Roses, love, apple trees, knowledge, doves, peace, corn, plenty, lilies, purity, honesty, honesty, bees, industry, sunflower and butterflies, hope. .
>
> The panels illustrate Shelley's line: "Hope will make thee young, for Hope and Youth are children of one mother, even Love."**

Time being short she quickly began work on the actual murals. She was assisted in the heavier manual work by R.C. Wallhead, of Wilmslow, a professional decorator and student of the Manchester Municipal School of Art who was later Labour MP for Merthyr Tydfil. The work, though that of a novice, seems to have satisfied its artistically untutored sponsors. Keir Hardie's *Labour Leader* described the hall as "tastefully decorated" and a true work of love.

Walter Crane came to speak at the opening ceremony, and Sylvia was asked to give a lecture on the principles of ornamentation and to explain her decorations. This was her first appearance on the platform, and she was so

---

* The foundation stone had been laid on November 26, 1898. *Salford Reporter*, December 3, 1898.

** From *The Revolt of Islam*, Canto 8, verse 27, lines 3434–5.

PLATE 1 Untitled. A fruit and vegetable stall in Venice.

PLATE II Untitled. A young woman painting decorations onto wooden ornamental plaques.

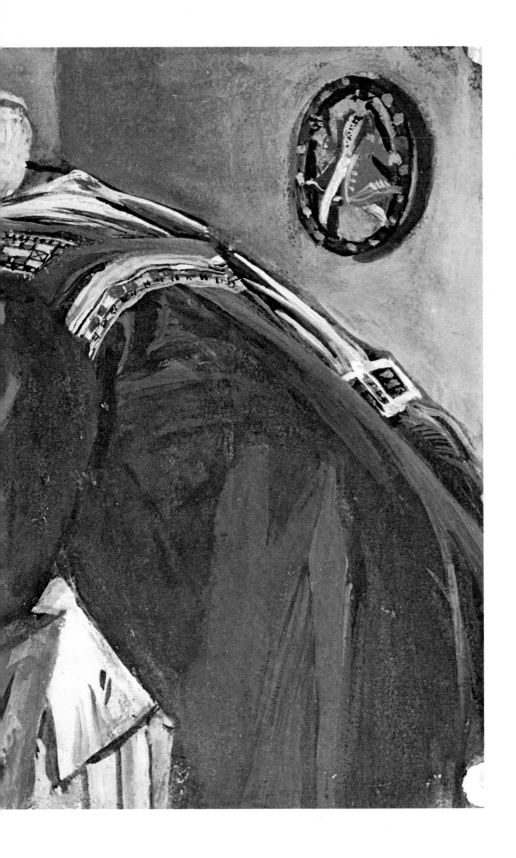

PLATE III Untitled. A small boy in an Italian street.

nervous that when drawing on the blackboard she forgot to remove her gloves.[5]

Sylvia's work on Pankhurst Hall by a quirk of history had important, though totally unexpected consequences both for her family and for the entire women's movement in Britain. While decorating the building she learned that women were not permitted to join that branch of the ILP as the organisation had decided that it should be a social club open only to men whether members of the ILP or not. The presence of women was therefore considered undesirable. It was indeed a paradox that the young Socialist party, following a tradition it might well have repudiated, had decided unashamedly to discriminate against women in a building decorated by a woman and named in honour of one of the chief advocates of women's emancipation. The Doctor's family was, not surprisingly, outraged, and the incident caused Mrs. Pankhurst to decide on establishing a new women's organisation.

On October 10, 1903, half a dozen ILP women were invited to Mrs. Pankhurst's house at 62 Nelson Street where they formed the Women's Labour Representation Committee. Finding that the name had already been appropriated it was, however, immediately changed to the Women's Social and Political Union which was soon known for short as the WSPU. Though at first conceived as an auxiliary to the Labour movement, to secure justice for women within the party, it was soon to develop an entirely independent existence, and in the next few years led its members – Sylvia, her sisters Christabel and Adela and their mother Mrs. Pankhurst not excluded – along entirely untrodden paths.

For the meantime, however, the young artist's life was little changed. She spent much of her time drawing, but, living with her mother, and with her sister Christabel studying law, she took on many responsibilities she had not known in Venice – housekeeping, dusting and darning. She also still wrote tickets for the shop, where she sold designs for cotton prints and some of the works she had painted in now far away Venice.

❧ 4 The Royal College of Art; Austin Spare; Early Suffragette Activity

T HOUGH SYLVIA HAD RETURNED TO MANCHESTER in the belief that she would have to help her mother it was soon apparent that the latter had little need of her, the more so as Mrs. Pankhurst had lost interest in her shop and was becoming increasingly involved in women's affairs. Sylvia, encouraged by her success with Pankhurst Hall, therefore decided to apply for a two-year national scholarship for the Royal College of Art at South Kensington.

The scholarship was based on a series of exams, the first of which was in geometry. Although she knew all the answers she was so nervous that she did not complete any of them. Her fingers shook, she dropped her ruler, and in making erasures almost rubbed holes into the paper. She went home in despair. She found the house closed, her mother, sisters and brother having all gone to the theatre. She nevertheless got in through a window and sadly went to bed. Having failed, as she assumed, she completed the rest of the exams with no further nervousness. It was later announced that she had first-class grades in every subject but geometry, and that her total marks had entirely compensated for her deficiency in that paper. She not only won the scholarship, but obtained the highest mark of any competitor. She was surprised, but not elated, for the standard, she concluded, could not have been very high. The thought of being able to devote the next two years to the study and creation of beauty nevertheless filled her with great excitement.

Sylvia, the young Mancunian art student, was far lonelier in the impersonal vastness of London than she had ever been in Venice. Her first weeks at South Kensington were moreover far from happy. A regulation had been made in the previous year that all students had to spend their first six months of the day course in studying architecture, life drawing being relegated to the evening. Wishing to devote much more time to the latter subject, she requested an interview with the principal, Mr. Spencer, to ask whether she and others with similar interests could not work in the day on the study of the human figure, which she felt so important, and leave architecture to the evening. The principal was unimpressed by her appeal and brusquely ordered her from his room. Had he argued that a decorative painter needed a knowledge of architecture, or that the resources of the college would not allow of the arrangement she had proposed she might have been convinced, but, as it was, she resented his manners, and thereafter when she and he met they glared at each other, as she afterwards recalled, like savage dogs.[1]

Another source of conflict arose from her discovery that there was considerable discrimination at the college against women students in the allocation of scholarships and prizes. Though in examinations outside the college the identity of the student was not known to the judges and the competition was therefore fair, in the college itself the principal made the final decision. The result, it appeared, was that though many women entered the college with scholarships few of them received further ones.

It was indeed normal practice in the painting school each year to award only one internal scholarship to a woman. Indignant at this she persuaded Keir Hardie to raise the matter in the House of Commons. In response to a parliamentary question in August 1905, he was informed that out of sixteen scholarships only three were awarded to women, and the authorities did "not contemplate any change" in the conditions under which they were granted. Sylvia and her friends were by no means satisfied, for they were sure that the ratio had no relation to the actual proportion of merit between the sexes in the college. That Miss Pankhurst had been responsible for the question in the House soon reached the principal's ear.

She, and indeed most of the other students, also had other causes for depression. They found, particularly in their first year, that the teachers were far less sympathetic than those in the local schools they had earlier attended, and she for her part was sad that she received none of the genial encouragement which had been a feature at the Manchester school, but rather scathing criticism.

Like most of the other students moreover she was in poor financial circumstances, for the scholarship, fifty pounds a year, plus travelling expenses from the student's home town, a stipend paid at the rate of five pounds per month during the term, necessitated the strictest economy, the more so as first year students had to purchase their own materials. She was also worried about the rent of the studio in Manchester which her mother had obtained for her, as well as about the financial position at home in general.

Her rent at this time was ten shillings a week for a miserable room in a tall house off the Fulham Road. Most students economised by sharing rooms. But in Sylvia's case her two best friends were outside the college: her brother Harry who was at school in Hampstead, and Keir Hardie in the House of Commons.

Though on distant terms of acquaintance with several groups and numerous individuals at the college, she was somewhat shy, and very much immersed in her study and politics, and therefore made no special friends at the college. For this reason some of the students considered her haughty, though she insisted that this was not the case, only that having outside interests she did not take the trouble to make the first advances on would-be friends. There were college dances every three weeks, as well as an annual fancy-dress ball on the preparation for which many students spent their spare time for several months. Sylvia, however, never went to them, though she did go to the occasional college concert.

Perhaps her best friend at college was Austin Osman Spare, a pale, flaxen-haired youth who dressed in a white shirt with a yellow sash. On account of the strangeness of his work he was regarded by many of the first year women students as a dangerous person although he was younger than any of them, only about eighteen years of age. They learned that he was about to publish a book of allegorical and satirical drawings entitled *Earth Inferno: Destiny, Humanity and the Chaos of Creation*, and was trying to sell advance copies of it. Sylvia told her fellow girl students that she was going to order one. Several of them, reluctant to approach him directly, asked her to do so on their behalf.*

She remained in intermittent contact with Spare long after she left the RCA. He supported some of her activities, notably her championing of Ethiopia, on occasion sending her some of his works to sell for charitable purposes – and when she went to live in Addis Ababa she took with her three paintings of this artist whom she always spoke of as one of the finest draughtsmen she had ever known.

Another friend she made at this time was a woman student, Amy Browning, who, as we shall see, was later to help her in several artistic matters.

Most of her fellow students, she found, suffered from anxieties not unknown to other generations of young artists, but particularly serious in the case of women in the early twentieth century who had limited employment opportunities open to them. Students of both sexes dreaded the time when their scholarships ended and they would be faced with the task of earning their

---

* This book, which seems amazingly modern even today, was printed by the Cooperative Printing Society in February 1905, and had an edition limited to two hundred and sixty-five copies.

living in an uncertain profession. The more ambitious feared that they would be obliged to abandon creative work in favour of teaching, while the less confident were afraid that they might not even find jobs as teachers. The girls, in particular, knew that they were seriously handicapped in that field for the best posts would go to men, even if less qualified than themselves. Such anxieties were reinforced by news of the difficulties which previous years' graduates were encountering. It was likewise apparent that their work was deteriorating under the necessity of having to do trade work for money, without the possibility of employing models or devoting sufficient time to study. Though some eventually freed themselves from penury many failed to do so, and it was perhaps little wonder that Sylvia knew of no less than five cases of insanity among the men students.

Realisation of these difficulties reinforced her belief in the evils of capitalism, and the need for a transformation of society on Socialist principles. Socialism, for her, as for many of her friends at this time, was not just an "ism" to speak of in the parlour, but the ultimate goal of social evolution to which mankind was inexorably advancing, a goal which could, and must, be achieved consciously through struggle and sacrifice.

Though conscious of the financial problems of the students, which she herself encountered, Sylvia also saw that she, and they, were in a privileged position in relation to the mass of the population, not only because, unlike so many, she had enough to eat, but also because she was engaged in work which gave her satisfaction. Considering this state of affairs as a Socialist concerned with how an ideal society should be organised, she once asked Keir Hardie: "Are we brothers of the brush entitled to the luxury of release from utilitarian production? Is it just that we should be permitted to devote our entire lives to the creation of beauty, while others are meshed in monotonous drudgery?"[2]

She maintained throughout her life a keen interest in struggling young artists. I remember once travelling with her late at night in the London Underground – she must by then have been in her sixties. She was very tired, but when a young French art student, obviously down-at-heel, entered with his girl friend, carrying a large portfolio of drawings, and sat down nearby, she crossed the compartment and got into animated conversation with him, examined his work with great care, and offered him much encouragement.

Sylvia's life in London soon developed a routine. She worked at the college from Monday to Friday, then on Saturday mornings went to the City to sell her designs for cotton prints. She was paid in guineas out of which she retained the shillings for her bus fares, and sent the pounds to her mother to whom she wrote more or less every other day. Sundays she often spent with her brother Harry who was free from his school every other week. Sometimes they visited Aunt Mary (by now Mrs. Clarke) in a dreary southeast London suburb, and other times Keir Hardie at his rooms at 14 Nevill's Court, an Elizabethan building said to be the oldest inhabited house in London. Describing the old man's house through her artistic eyes, always interested in detail, she recalls that:

A dark winding stair led to his dwelling in that narrow alley off Fetter Lane. It had originally been one large room, but was divided, partly by partitions, partly by a curtain, into a living room, a bedroom and a tiny box of a kitchen. The woodwork, which reached nearly to the ceiling, was painted dark green. There was a narrow seat, and a high, old-fashioned fireplace with hobs on either side. On the walls were engravings framed in polished rosewood: an excellent representation of one of the great franchise demonstrations of 1867, a charming portrait of Robert Owen in a circular frame, portraits of William Morris and Robert Burns, a bas-relief of Walt Whitman and some paintings by Socialist comrades. On the high narrow mantelpiece were a bust of Emerson and a little iron figure of Dr. Johnson. A polished table by the door held a collection of curios, mostly old silver. Beside his big chair was a standard lamp draped with the Union Jack, a trophy captured from invading jingoes at one of his meetings against the South African war. The lamp was not used, for he preferred always to work by candlelight. To see him here came people of all sorts and stations; Socialists and social reformers, people from India and the small nations, Russian exiles, writers, painters, musicians, dreamers of dreams, to whom the legend of this man was an inspiration and a light.

He lived with extreme frugality, cooking his food, doing his housework, blacking his boots, be it said with care, for he was a model of cleanly neatness. An old woman came to char for a few hours each week; for the rest he looked after himself. He had a marvellous way with him in lighting a fire. As a miner he had made a collection of fossils he found in the workings, and he seemed to have a very affection for the coal itself. He liked "the grip of it", he told me, but he was always scrupulous in washing his hands immediately after touching it. I have seen him come home on a cold, dark evening after an arduous day, strip off his overcoat, go to the fireplace, and light a fire on the top of the spent coals in the grate. In a few moments there would be a cheerful blaze. Then he would bring forth bread, butter and Scotch scones, the main staples of his diet, and tea, which he would often cast into a saucepan of cold water, taking it off the fire as soon as it came to the boil. After this simple repast, he would light his pipe and seat himself for a chat; a brief one, for work was always a claimant. Soon he would turn to his letters, or an article, giving me a book to read, and perhaps asking me to mark and annotate the salient passages, or it might be a printer's proof to correct. Books were his chief companions, and if work was not too pressing, he would lay it aside for a time and read aloud: Shelley, Byron, William Morris, Scott, Shakespeare, Walt Whitman – his taste was catholic; Robbie Burns was probably nearest his heart; Keats was another special favourite. He was intensely interested in modern writers who dealt with social questions; Ibsen, Anatole France, Galsworthy, Shaw. My first winter in London, Shaw's *John Bull's Other Island* was produced at the Court Theatre; we saw it together. Afterwards we took a meal at a nearby restaurant. When I asked for black coffee, which he had never tasted, he was as much astonished, he told me later, as though I had 'called for a cigar'. This was saying a good deal, for few women smoked in those days, and fewer still outside the privacy of their homes. Inspired by my example, he afterwards adopted black coffee as his favourite beverage; one of the very few indulgences he permitted himself.[3]

It was probably at about this time that she began an impressionistic water-colour portrait of her old Socialist friend, pipe in mouth (No. 10), which now hangs in the National Portrait Gallery, London, together with a later more detailed study (No. 46).

No. 10: Keir Hardie.

Hardie, she was later to declare, was ever "a buttress against cynicism and spiritual despair, for in the last essence, whether one is prosperous and successful is infinitely less important to the inner self than belief in mankind and its destiny wherein he never faltered."[4]

Sylvia, who was then living at Park Cottage, 45 Park Walk, Chelsea, had joined the Chelsea branch of the ILP in her first year in London. Not long afterwards she addressed her first women's suffrage meeting when she took the chair for the pioneer feminist Dora Montefiore at an open-air gathering in Ravenscourt Park. The art student's heart "thumped terribly", but the public proving sympathetic, she soon gained confidence, and subsequently recalled that the affair "seemed tame enough when over".[5]

Her landlady at Park Cottage was Mrs. Florence Roe, a warmhearted Cockney whose husband made riding breeches, and considered a Tory government best for business. But Sylvia soon converted him and his wife into enthusiastic supporters of Votes for Women and Socialism. She felt herself at home at the Roes', where she had two rooms, one of them empty and free from *bric-à-brac* in which she could paint. She often invited the women students of her year to sketch with her there on Saturday afternoons, when, to avoid the cost of employing models, one of them would pose for the rest.

Not long after moving into Park Cottage Sylvia was joined, in February 1905, by her mother who came down from Manchester for the opening of the parliamentary session. It was customary for MPs to draw lots for the right to introduce private members' bills, and Mrs. Pankhurst hoped to persuade one of the lucky few to move a women's suffrage bill. Her daughter dutifully absented herself from college to help in "lobbying". It was her first experience of this activity. She later observed that though she knew it would be "an uphill task", she had "no conception of how hard and discouraging it was to be". The MPs all declared that they had pledged themselves to do "something for their constituents", had some other measure in which they were interested, or had not been in Parliament long and preferred to wait until they had more experience before they would care to ballot for a bill at all. Yes, they were "in favour" of women's suffrage, but they could not give their places for the question.[6] Keir Hardie was therefore the women's only supporter.

Though not himself successful in the ballot, he succeeded in finding an MP willing to move a bill which was finally introduced in May. Mrs. Pankhurst and Sylvia then went around London to meetings to obtain signatures to a petition in support of it. When the great day came there were no longer, as in February, just two women lobbyists in the House – Sylvia and her mother – but

52

No. 11: Propaganda postcard.
The drawing was originally
designed for Keir Hardie's
proposed poster campaign for the
unemployed in 1905.

so many that the corridor and the passages approaching it were crowded. The
women were so numerous, in fact, that they believed victory in sight, and were
correspondingly dejected when they learned that the bill, which had been
discussed amid roars of laughter from its opponents, had been deliberately
"talked out" so that closing time came before it could be put to the vote.

Not long afterwards Sylvia obtained her first London commission, albeit
an unpaid one, when Keir Hardie asked her to design a coloured poster, as he
had conceived the idea of plastering the city with demands for the enactment
of the bill for the unemployed then before the House of Commons. He gave
her a weekend to execute the work. She undertook it with enthusiasm, but the
project had to be abandoned on account of the mutilation of the bill of 1905
by the Conservatives and Liberals who then controlled Parliament.[7]

FEED MY LAMBS.

No. 12: *Feed my Lambs.* A drawing used as a postcard.

Though the proposed poster campaign failed to materialise, the drawing (No. 11), which carried the monogram "E.S.P.", was turned into a propaganda postcard. A design of simplicity, but not without strength, it depicted a demonstration of workers led by a man in his shirtsleeves with a white shirt and brown trousers, and a woman in a red shawl and white apron, jointly clasping with determination a placard bearing the words, in black on white, "Workers are Hungry. Vote for the Bill". Behind it, and in front of a white and brown cloud, we can just see another poster, in orange on blue, which presumably reads, "We demand the Right to Work."

Sylvia's Socialist convictions and artistic conceptions also found expression at about this time in a simple pen and ink sketch (No. 12) of a resplendent woman clasping to her breast two youngsters who are apparently drinking from a pitcher of milk. The drawing, which was also used as a postcard, bears the E.S.P. monogram, and the forceful legend, "Feed my Lambs".

⚜ 5 Beginnings of Women's Militancy in Manchester and London; Artist or Social Reformer?

THE WOMEN'S SOCIAL AND POLITICAL UNION began its militant agitation in the autumn of 1905. It was generally regarded as a time when the political scene in Britain was in a state of flux. The return of a Liberal government was anticipated, and with it a new era of reform. All indications were, however, that, despite the lobbying of the newly established WSPU, the new government's legislation would not include any measure for women's enfranchisement.

Women's militancy began in Manchester while Sylvia was away in London as an art student. The Liberal statesman Sir Edward Grey went up to Manchester to address a meeting in the Free Trade Hall – site of the Peterloo massacre almost a century earlier – to explain the reforms which a Liberal government would introduce.

The WSPU, as a Manchester-based organisation, asked him to receive a women's deputation, but this, ominously, he refused to do. Christabel Pankhurst, then a student of law, and Annie Kenney, a cotton spinner from Lees near Oldham, accordingly went to the meeting on October 13 to ask what for the WSPU was the burning question: "Will the Liberal Government give women the vote?" Christabel, who remembered the tactics adopted by her family and others over the Boggart Hole Clough incident almost a decade earlier, went with the express intention of being arrested, and cheerfully declared, "I shall sleep in prison tonight!"

After Grey had spoken – without making any reference to women's emancipation – the two young women interrupted the proceedings to ask their soon to be famous question. No answer was vouchsafed. The two interrupters were duly expelled, and Annie Kenney was beaten up by the stewards. She and Christabel thereupon tried to hold a meeting of indignation outside the hall, but were speedily arrested.

Christabel was charged on the following day with spitting in the face of a police superintendent and an inspector. She was ordered to pay a fine of ten shillings or go to prison, while Annie Kenney had the choice of a fine of five shillings or three days in prison. Both chose to go to gaol. Christabel was later threatened with expulsion from her college and obliged to refrain from making further disturbances until she took her degree.

The Conservative government resigned a few weeks later, on December 4. The Liberals shortly afterwards called a great meeting at the Albert Hall where all their leaders were to be present. Annie Kenney came down to London to repeat her question, and stayed with Sylvia at Park Cottage. The organisers of the meeting allowed entry only by ticket. Because of the earlier incident in Manchester involving a "Miss Pankhurst", Sylvia was refused one, but later succeeded, with some difficulty, in obtaining three through Keir Hardie.

Since she was known as a Pankhurst, and would almost certainly be prevented from entering the hall, she confined herself to designing posters for her friends to display in the hall. Annie Kenney and two other women, however, gained admission, and asked their questions to which, as anticipated, they received no answer. Annie Kenney thereupon displayed a little white calico flag with the slogan "Votes for Women" painted on it in black letters, while at the other end of the hall another of the women, Theresa Billington, let down a nine foot banner which inquired "Will the Liberal Government give Justice to Working Women?" The questions and posters led to an uproar during which the three women were expelled.

On the following day Sylvia returned to Manchester for the Christmas vacation. Winston Churchill was also expected, as he was to speak at a number of meetings for the Liberals, and it was decided by the WSPU that its members should be present at all of them. He was selected for this attention as he was the most prominent Liberal candidate standing for a constituency within reach of the Pankhurst family.

To further the WSPU's agitation, banners were to be prepared bearing the words "Votes for Women" and "Will the Liberal Government give Women the Vote?" These texts, which were written in black on white calico, had to be repeated hundreds of times, since the banners would be snatched away as soon as they were displayed. Sylvia was naturally chosen for this tedious work. She was engaged on this "early and late, with scarcely any pause, throughout the festive days".[1]

She was herself present at the first of Churchill's meetings, which was held in a school in Cheetham Hill. She asked her question which the speaker attempted to ignore, but her brother Harry and another man at the back of the room led the audience in demanding that she should be answered. Such a clamour was raised that the speaker could not proceed. As soon as Sylvia rose to repeat the question there was silence, but when Churchill again failed to respond the din began once more. This continued for some time. The stewards wanted to throw her out, but were unable to do so as the hall was packed, and a number of the men sitting by her would not have tolerated any such action. To break the deadlock the chairman asked her to put her question from the platform. She then spoke for a few minutes, but could scarcely be heard above the general uproar. After this Churchill seized her, pushed her into a chair at the back of the platform, and insisted that she stay there until she had heard his reply. "Nothing", he declared, "would induce me to vote for giving women the franchise; I am not going to be henpecked."

Sylvia would have walked out then, but there was a scuffle in which the men on the platform stood up, thus hiding what was happening on the platform. She was seized by two of the organisers, and locked in an anteroom where one them abused her violently, calling her a cat, and gesticulating as though he would scratch her face with his hands. She succeeded, however, in opening a window through which she cried out to people passing in the street, "I want you to be a witness of anything that takes place in this room!" Some of the passers-by shouted to the man to behave himself. He thereupon left, locking her in the room, but she succeeded in escaping from the window, and at once held an impromptu meeting of protest – and gave the story to the Press thereby creating many jokes at the candidate's expense.

At Churchill's next meeting she was again present to ask her question and in fact she, her sister Adela, and Annie Kenney dogged him at every gathering he addressed in Manchester. My mother, it may be added, had a poor opinion of her erstwhile opponent throughout her life, and found herself on opposite sides with him on a number of issues, notably a generation or so later when he expressed strong support for Mussolini and Italian fascism which she vigorously opposed.[2] In 1945 when the Labour and Liberal parties, fearing to be seen opposing the former wartime leader, refrained from putting up candidates in his constituency, Woodford, and explained to the electorate that they could not "vote for Churchill" unless they resided there, she, happening to be one of his constituents, created a minor stir by announcing that she would cast her ballot for an independent, somewhat crankish candidate whose prime, almost sole claim for support was that he was standing against the Tory premier.

The general election of 1906 resulted, as expected, in the formation of a Liberal government, but also in the arrival in Parliament of twenty-nine Labour MPs and hence the creation of the Labour party – "our party" as Sylvia considered it. After the polls she returned to the Royal College of Art in a mood of joyous exhilaration.

She could, however, no longer devote herself wholeheartedly to her studies, because agitation for women's enfranchisement was soon in full stride. Annie Kenney arrived a few days later to "rouse London", and again stayed with her. There were no more Saturday painting parties in Park Cottage, for her rooms were thereafter used almost entirely for suffrage meetings. The young artist who had been horribly nervous when selling her designs found that in fighting for the women's cause all fears had gone.[3]

After rushing to Keir Hardie for advice, she rented the Caxton Hall for London's first militant women's meeting, went to the East End to get in touch with its Socialist leader George Lansbury to organise a women's suffrage procession, and ran about Fleet Street at night delivering letters to the Press to introduce the "mill hand who had gone to prison for the vote"; since she had no typewriter she had written these by hand. The *Daily Mail,* which at this time gave the militant women some publicity, coined for them the name "Suffragettes". Sylvia became the honorary secretary of the London-based national committee of the WSPU, the other members being her Aunt Mary, and her landlady Mrs. Roe. Mrs. Emmeline Pethick Lawrence who joined them shortly afterwards, to become the honorary treasurer, later recalled that Sylvia was then a "quiet and a shy" girl.[4]

As the time for the Caxton Hall meeting, on February 16, approached, she once again turned her attention to the preparation of banners. She purchased a supply of white linen, and in her sitting room in Park Cottage produced banners in Indian ink to be taken in procession to the House of Commons.

Mrs. Pankhurst, who came down to London for the event, stayed with her, together with another suffragist, Mrs. Nellie Martel. Sylvia's mother feared that her daughter had been unwise in hiring so large a hall, as she doubted whether they would be able to fill it. When the time came, however, it was easily packed, many women who were not yet supporters coming in disguise to hear what the Suffragettes had to say. After the meeting the audience streamed to the House of Commons: "It was bitterly cold and pouring with rain," Sylvia was later to recall, "but when we arrived at the Strangers' Entrance, we found that for the first time that anyone could remember, the door of the House of Commons was closed to women. Cards were sent in to several

Private Members, some of whom came out and urged that we be allowed to enter, but the government had given its orders, and the police remained obdurate. All the women refused to go away, and permission was finally given for twenty women at a time to be admitted. Then hour after hour the women stood outside in the rain to enter. Some of them never got into the House at all."[5]

In the months which followed the little rooms in Park Cottage continued to be the centre of the militant women's movement, and on the subsequent appointment of Theresa Billington as a WSPU organiser she too came to live there.

Not long afterwards, on April 25, Keir Hardie attempted to move a women's suffrage resolution in the House of Commons. Sylvia was among a group of Suffragettes who went to the House to watch the proceedings, which ended with the resolution being "talked out" by its opponents, and thus not put to a vote. Members of the WSPU, angered by the repetition of this manoeuvre, protested from the Strangers' Gallery, and were roughly dragged out by the police. It was, she recalled, "with a feeling almost of triumph that we cried shame upon the men who had wasted hours in useless talk and pitiful and pointless jokes with which to insult our country-women."[6]

Undeterred by this defeat the WSPU held its first big open-air meeting a few weeks later in Trafalgar Square in May. Surveying the platform not so much as the honorary secretary of the WSPU but as an artist, she later described the Suffragette leaders in a vivid account which reveals her interest in pictorial detail.

In my mind's eye I can clearly see the chairman, my mother, with her pale face, her quiet dark clothes, her manner calm, as it always is on such great occasions, and her quiet-sounding but far-reaching voice with its plaintive minor chords. I can see beside her the strangely diverse group of speakers: Theresa Billington in her bright blue dress, strongly built and upstanding, her bare head crowned with those brown coils of wonderfully abundant hair. I see Keir Hardie, in his rough homespun jacket, with his deep-set, honest eyes, and his face full of human kindness, framed by the halo of his silver hair. Then Mrs. Elmy, fragile, delicate and wonderfully sweet, with her face looking like a tiny bit of finely modelled, finely tinted porcelain, her shining dark brown eyes and her long grey curls. Standing very close to her is Annie Kenney, whose soft bright hair falls loosely from her vivid sensitive face, and hangs down her back in a long plait, just as she wore it in the cotton mill. Over her head she wears a green shawl as she did in Lancashire, and pinned to her white blouse is a brilliant red rosette, showing her to be one of the marshals of the procession, whilst her dark blue serge skirt just shows the steel tips of her clogs. How beautiful they are, these two women, as hand clasped in hand they stand before us! – one rich in the mellow sweetness of old age which crowns a life of long toil for the common good; the other filled with a chivalrous youth; both dedicated to a great reform.[7]

Some weeks later Annie Kenney, Adela Pankhurst and several other women were arrested for Suffragette agitation in both London and Manchester. Sylvia, shocked by the news, records that she and most of her friends at that time still "knew little of the interior of the prison, but on those burning July days, we knew enough to think with sorrow and anxiety of our comrades shut away from the beauty of the summer in the heat of their small, stifling cells." She and the other Suffragettes nonetheless "heard with joy" that the detainees were "happy and contented to suffer imprisonment for the women's cause".[8]

Sylvia's two-year scholarship at the Royal College of Art came to an end in the summer of 1906. Almost every moment free from her college work had been devoted to the WSPU so no time had been left to prepare any way of earning her living. Her teachers in the school of painting had advised her to apply for a free studentship to complete the five-year course so as to take the diploma, but she did not do so, for, involved as she was in the movement, she saw no possibility of supporting herself as a student. Having over-worked for so long she was moreover in poor health and suffering again from neuralgia. She suggested to her mother that she be relieved of her honorary secretaryship of the WSPU in order to seek employment, but Mrs. Pankhurst insisted that she should not do so until Christabel could complete her studies and thus be free to come to London. However, her mother did not favour full-time employment for her with the WSPU for Christabel and Adela were already both paid organisers, and she felt it was undesirable for more of her family to be on the society's payroll.

Sylvia had no wish to become a paid employee of the Union, as she was beginning to feel doubts as to its leadership. Though loving her mother, and admiring Christabel – she recalled their happiness together as children – she "detested" the latter's "incipient Toryism" and was later to deplore the "frequent casting out of trusty friends for a mere hair's breadth difference of view". For the time being, however, she refrained from crossing swords with Christabel, in part because she felt herself as "one who had come into active political life only as a sacrifice to the urgency of the need, departing from the path I had marked out for myself, and to which it was then my intention to return".[9]

60

Above all, Sylvia's dream was still to be not a political activist or organiser, but an artist, albeit one working in the cause of social progress. Realising that the constantly increasing activities of the WSPU required more and more the services of a full-time secretary, and that Christabel would soon be coming to London, she finally wrote a letter of resignation, and carried off her drawing-board and materials to the rooms of a fellow student. Soon afterwards for eleven shillings a week she rented two unfurnished rooms in Cheyne Walk, on the Embankment, next door to the house formerly occupied by the artist Turner. She was still so racked with pain that it took her nearly a week to pack her belongings. Then she hired a youth with a handcart to transport her campbed, easel, cases of books and paints, and one small bag of clothes to Cheyne Walk.

Artistic and even literary work was, however, difficult to come by, particularly for a known Suffragette whose cause was then being vilified in the popular Press. When she called at the offices of magazines there was always a titter when her name was given. If editors agreed to see her they assumed that she wanted to write about votes for women, and were then unwilling to devote much space to the subject, let alone to pay for it. They seemed unable to believe that she could do anything outside the strictly women's field. Eventually she obtained several remunerative jobs, including a commission, through Keir Hardie, for two illuminated addresses, and subsequently wrote a series of paid articles on women's affairs under the pen-name "Ignota" for the *Westminster Review,* a Liberal journal once edited by J.S.Mill.

As an artist she was not interested in purely commercial art, and soon realised that it was impossible to undertake the mammoth works of art for which she yearned. Sir William Richmond, who had earlier given her great encouragement when he had seen her paintings at the Royal College of Art, and whom she met at about this time, told her frankly that though large decoration was his ideal also, no one could live by it, as the few persons in a position to commission it did not care for it.

There was in addition for her the inner problem more poignant than any other, "whether it was worthwhile to fight one's individual struggle, as fight one must, and that strenuously, to make one's way as an artist, to bring out of oneself the best possible, and to induce the world to accept one's creations, and give one in return one's daily bread, when all the time the great struggles to better the world for humanity demanded other service." And yet, despite that, "the idea of giving up the artist's life, surrendering the study of colour and form, laying aside the beloved pigments and brushes, to wear out one's life on the platform and the chair at the street corner was a prospect too tragically grey and barren to endure".[10]

Her doubts and uncertainties notwithstanding she remained a keen supporter of the WSPU and enthusiastically designed its membership card (Plate XIII). One of her first artistic works for the movement, and in many ways reminiscent of her poster for the unemployed, the card was apparently conceived towards the end of 1906 or early 1907; it was a gouache, printed in bright colours. It depicted a procession of women workers in clogs, one carrying a pail and the other a baby. The figure in front holds up a scroll-like banner against a blue sky with the words, "Votes. Votes. Votes".

6 Two Imprisonments in Holloway; Prison Sketches; Drawings for the WSPU

SYLVIA'S FIRST IMPRISONMENT left a vivid impression on her. It began on October 24, 1906, less than a year after her first encounter with Winston Churchill at the Free Trade Hall in Manchester. The Suffragettes had demonstrated outside the House of Commons on the previous day, and entering the lobby in small groups had conducted an illegal meeting there, after which ten women, including her younger sister Adela and Mrs. Annie Cobden Sanderson had been arrested. The detention of the latter was to have significant consequences and created considerable excitement as she was the daughter of the Anti-Corn Leaguer Richard Cobden, one of the founders of British liberalism, and a woman of distinction as all who knew her were aware. Sylvia, who was impressed by her quiet dignity, later described her in words which both rebut the popular modern conception of the Suffragettes as "battle-axes", and reveal something of her own artistic interests:

> You must not picture her as being either big-boned, plain-looking and aggressive and wearing "mannish" clothes, or as emotional and overstrung. On the contrary, she is just what Reynolds, Hoppner, Sir Henry Raeburn, or Romney with his softest and tenderest touch, would have loved to paint. Not very tall, she is comfortably and firmly knit and as she walks she puts her foot down quite firmly, in a dignified and stately way. She is always dressed in low-toned greys and lilacs, and her clothes are gracefully and delicately wrought, with all sorts of tiny tuckings and finishings which give a suggestion of daintiest detail without any loss of simplicity or breadth. She has a shower of hair like spun silver that crinkles itself in the most original and charming way, and which she winds around with broad ribbon, lest its loose falling strands should mar the neatness of her aspect. Her cheeks are tinged with the soft dull rose that one sees in pastel, and her eyes have the most genial and benevolent glance.[1]

On appearing in the court Mrs. Cobden Sanderson told the magistrate, in her calm quiet voice, that she had gone to the House of Commons to demand the vote; that as long as women were deprived of citizen's rights and had, therefore, no constitutional means of obtaining redress, they had a right to make themselves heard by other means. She went on to quote John Burns, then a member of the Liberal government, who had earlier declared, "I am a law-breaker because I desire to be a law-maker." Her speech, which supporters of the Liberal government found exceedingly embarrassing, was frequently interrupted by the magistrate who, refusing to hear the defence of any of the accused, briskly ordered them all to promise to keep the peace for six months, failing which they would be sent to prison for two months in the second division.* The women protested at not being permitted to speak, and declared that they would not leave the court until they had been granted the right to which all accused were allowed, namely to make a statement in their own defence, but the magistrate, unmoved by this plea, called the police to have them removed by force.

Sylvia was indignant that ten earnest women had been thus hustled off to prison after a trial lasting less than half an hour. She walked into the court and complained to the magistrate that women, even those desirous of giving evidence, had been excluded from gaining admission. She was at once dragged out, and thrown into the street. There she tried to address the crowd, but was promptly seized and charged with obstruction and abusive language. Back in court she protested against the latter charge, which was immediately withdrawn, but was sentenced on the former to pay a fine of one pound or undergo a fortnight's imprisonment, in the third, or worst, division. Choosing the latter alternative she was driven off in a black van to Holloway Prison. Later she recalled the experience:

> How long the way seemed to Holloway, as the springless van rattled over the stones and constantly bumped us against the narrow wooden pens in which we sat! As it passed down the poor streets the people cheered – they always cheer the prison van. It was evening when we arrived at our destination, and the darkness was closing in. As we passed in a single file through the great gates, we found ourselves at the end of a long corridor with cubicles on either side. A woman officer in a holland dress, with a dark blue bonnet with hanging strings on her head, and with a bundle of keys and chains jangling at her waist, called out our names and the length of our sentences and locked us separately into one of the cubicles, which were about four feet square and quite dark. In the door of each cubicle was a little round glass spy-hole, which might be closed by a metal flap on the outside. Mine had been left open by mistake, and through it I could see a little of what was going on outside.

---

* There were three types of imprisonment in British prisons: first division, afforded to political prisoners, who could receive unrestricted correspondence and visits, and practise their profession; second division, in which prisoners could write and receive a letter but monthly; and third division, in which this could be done only after the first two months. The diet in the three divisions also varied greatly.

Once we had been locked away, the wardress came from door to door, taking down further particulars as to the profession, religion, and so on, of each prisoner … . The prisoners called to each other over the tops of the cubicles in loud, high pitched voices. Every now and then the officer protested, but still the noise continued. Soon another van load of prisoners arrived and the cubicles being filled, several women together were put into the same compartment – sometimes as many as five in one of those tiny places ! It was very cold, and the stone floor made one's feet colder still, yet for a long time until I was so tired that I could no longer stand – I was afraid to sit down because, in the darkness, one could not see whether, as one feared, everything might be covered with vermin.[2]

The prisoners were then ordered to undress, to put on a short cotton chemise, and told to surrender their money, and jewellery which were duly registered for subsequent return. They were then commanded to take a bath, after which they had to dress themselves in prison clothes, which, she recalls, were "badly sewn and badly cut", and made of "coarse calico and harsh woollen stuff", with "innumerable strings to fasten round one's waist. A strange-looking pair of corsets was supplied to each of us, but these we were not obliged to wear unless we wished. The stockings were of harsh thick wool, and had been badly darned. They were black with red stripes going around the legs, and as they were very wide, and there were no garters or suspenders to keep them up, they were constantly slipping down and wrinkling around one's ankles."

On opening her door she found that outside all was hurry and confusion. In the dim light the women were scrambling for dresses lying like heaps on the floor.

The skirts of these dresses – like the petticoats, of which there were three – were of the same width at both top and bottom, and they were gathered into wide bands which, though fastened with tapes were not made to draw up, and had to be over-lapped in the most clumsy fashion in order to make them fit any but the very stoutest women. The bodices were so strangely cut that even when worn by very thin people they seemed bound to gape in front, especially as they were fastened with only one button at the neck. My bodice, the only one I could manage to get hold of, had several large rents, which had been roughly cobbled together with black cotton. Every article of clothing was conspicuously stamped with the broad arrow, which was painted black on light garments, and white on those which were dark.

She had scarcely fastened her dress when someone called to the prisoners to put on their shoes which were bundled together on a rack. None of them seemed to be in pairs, and they were heavy and clumsy, with leather laces that broke easily in the hand. The last articles of the prisoners' attire were "white cotton caps fastened under the chin with strings and stamped in black with the broad arrow, and the blue and check white aprons and handkerchief, both of which looked like dusters".

She and her comrades were then led off on an almost interminable journey to their cells.

> It seemed a sort of skeleton building that we were taken through – the strangest place in which I had ever been. In every great oblong ward or block through which we passed, though there were many storeys, one could see right down to the basement and up to the lofty roof. The stone floors of the corridors lined the walls all the way round, jutting out at the junctions of the storeys like shelves some nine or ten feet apart, being protected on the outer edge by an iron wire trellis work four or five feet high, and having on the wall side rows and rows and rows of numbered doors studded with nails. The various storeys were connected by flights of iron steps bordered by iron trellis work, and reaching in slanting lines from corridor to corridor. All the walls and doors were painted stone colour and all the iron work was painted black.
>
> We clattered up those seemingly endless flights and shuffled along those mazy corridors in our heavy shoes and at last stopped at a small office ... where our names and the length of our sentences and all the various other particulars were verified once more, and the sheets for the bed, a Bible and a number of other little books with black shiny bindings were given to us.

After another long march through prison corridors a wardress with jangling keys unlocked a number of heavy iron doors, and having ordered one prisoner into each cell, pulled each door closed with a loud bang.

> I now found myself in a small whitewashed cell twelve or thirteen feet long by seven feet wide and about nine feet high. The floor was of stone. The window, which was high up near the ceiling, had many little panes enclosed in a heavy iron frame-work and guarded by strong iron bars outside. The iron door was studded with nails and its round eye-like spy-hole was now covered on the outside. On the left-hand side of the door was a small recess, some four feet from the ground, in which, behind a pane of thick opaque glass, was a flickering gas jet which cast a dim light into the cell. Under this recess was a small wooden shelf, somewhere about fourteen or fifteen inches square, which I afterwards learned was called a table, and opposite this was a wooden stool. On the floor, leaning against the wall under the window, were arranged a number of utensils made of black tin, these being a plate, a small water can holding about three pints of water, a tiny shallow wash-basin less than a foot in diameter, and a small slop-pail with a lid. Two little round brushes, in shape rather like those we use for brushing clothes, which were intended for sweeping the floor, a little tin dust pan, and a piece of bath-brick wrapped in some rags for cleaning the tins. These also were all placed in an order which, as I soon learned, was never to be changed. A small towel and a smaller

tablecloth, both of them resembling dish cloths, hung on a nail. Propped against
the right-hand wall was the plank bed, with the pillow balanced on top. The bed
is, I think, two feet six inches in width, and when in position for sleeping is raised
up by two cross pieces to about two inches from the floor.

While she was still examining all these things in wonder her door was opened,
and a wardress sharply exclaimed, "What, have you not made your bed yet ?
The light will be put out soon. You had better make haste !" The young
Suffragette prisoner asked for a nightdress, but this was refused. The iron door
was then once more banged shut, and she was left alone to sleep. This was,
however, "one of the hardest things to obtain in Holloway. The bed is so hard,
the blankets and sheets are scarcely wide enough to cover one, and the pillow,
filled with a kind of herb, seems as if it were made of stone. The window is not
made to open. The system of ventilation is exceedingly bad, and though one is
usually cold at night one always suffers terribly from want of air."[3]

Each morning while it was still dark she would be awakened by the tramp
of heavy feet and the ringing of bells, after which the light was turned on. She
had then to wash in the tiny basin and dress hurriedly. Soon she would hear the
rattle of keys and the clanging of heavy iron doors coming nearer and nearer
until it reached her own door. When this was opened a wardress would order
her sharply: "Empty your slops, twelve !" – the number by which she was
designated. She would hasten to do so, and then returned to her cell at the
word of command.

Then, just as she had been instructed, she rolled her bed. The first sheet
had to be folded in four, then spread out on the floor, and rolled up from one
end, tightly, like a sausage. The second sheet had to be rolled round it, and
round this, one by one, the blankets and quilt. Prisoners had to do this very
neatly if they were not to be reprimanded.

Next she had to clean her tins. She had to take three pieces of rag with
which to do this. Two of them were frayed scraps of brown serge, like the
prison dress, and the third a piece of white calico. These rags were not new,
having been used by previous occupants of the cell. Folded up in these rags was
a piece of bathbrick which had to be rubbed on the stone floor until a quantity
of dust had been removed. She had then to take one of the brown rags and rub
this on to the yellow cake of soap also used for her face. With this soapy rag
she had to rub over one of the tins, and then dip the rag into the brick dust
which was lying on the floor, and rub it on the soapy tin. Then she had to rub
it again with the second brown rag, and polish with the white calico one. All
the tins had to be scoured very bright.

Not long afterwards the door would open and shut again, and she would be left a pail of water with which she had to scrub the stool, bed and table, and then the floor. All this was supposed to be done before breakfast, though it often took her much longer.

Before she had finished the work there would be another jangling of keys and clanging of iron doors. "Where's your pint, twelve?" She would hand it out, spread her little cloth, and set her plate ready. Her pint pot was then filled with gruel (oatmeal and water without any seasoning – for which reason perhaps she was to hate porridge as long as I can remember), and some six pieces of bread would be thrust on to her plate. Then the door closed. After this she would eat her breakfast, and then, if her cleaning was done, begin to sew. She would usually have sheets to make and was expected, according to her work card, to produce fifteen per week.

At half-past eight she and the other prisoners would be put in a line and marched out to chapel. A wardress watched to see that no one spoke, and issued a battery of commands and criticism: "Tie up your cap string, twenty-seven. You look like a cinder-picker. You must learn to dress decently here." "Hold up your head, thirty. Hurry up, twenty-three." On reaching the chapel Sylvia herself might receive a rebuke, "Don't look about you, twelve." After this the clergymen entered, read the lessons, and conducted prayers and hymns. Then back to the cells.

At twelve o'clock came "dinner": a pint of oatmeal porridge and six ounces of bread three days a week, six ounces of suet pudding and six ounces of bread twice a week, and on two other days eight ounces of potatoes and six ounces of bread.

After this meal the prisoners remained in their cells for the rest of the day, except to fetch water between two and three o'clock, although three days a week they were also sent for exercise. On such occasions the women, dressed in drab-coloured capes, marched slowly round in single file, a distance of three or four yards between them to prevent communication. Two of the very oldest women, who could only totter along, went up and down at one side, passing and repassing each other.

Despite such monotonous discipline the artist-prisoner looked forward to such brief periods of exercise, and was filled with excitement to see the sun.

If you come into prison on Wednesday, the first day for you to exercise will be Saturday. How long it seems since you were last in the outside world, since you saw the sky and the sunshine and felt the pure fresh air against your cheek! How vividly everything strikes you now. Every detail stands out in your mind with never-to-be-forgotten clearness. Perhaps it is a showery autumn day. The blue sky is flecked with quickly driving clouds. The sun shines brightly and lights up the puddles on the ground and the raindrops still hanging from the eaves and window ledges. The wind comes in little playful gusts. The free pigeons are flying about in happy confidence. You notice every variation in their glossy plumage. Some are grey with purple throats, some have black markings on their wings, some are a pale brown colour, some nearly white; one is a deep purple, almost black, with shining white bars on his wings and tail. All are varied – no two are alike. The gaunt prison buildings surround everything, but in all this shimmering brightness, in this sweet, free air, they have lost for a moment their gloomy terror.

[Soon, however] your eye lights on your fellow prisoners. You are brought back to the dreary truth of prison life. With measured tread, and dull listless step, they shuffle on. Their heads are bent, their eyes cast down. They do not see the sun and the brightness, the precious sky or the hovering birds. They do not even see the ground at their feet, for they pass over sunk stones, through wet and mud, though there be dry ground on either side. They have lost hope, and the sight of nature has no power to make them glad. It may be that when next you walk with them you will feel as they do. These gloomy overshadowing walls and the remembrance of your narrow cell, with its endless twilight and dreary, useless tasks may have filled your mind and driven away all other thoughts.

Back in their cells the prisoners' last meal at five o'clock was six ounces of bread and a pint of gruel. Not long afterwards the lights went out, and then followed another long sleepless night with "the awakening to another day like yesterday and like to-morrow."[4]

Sylvia suffered this soul-destroying routine for eight days, during which time outside the prison Keir Hardie, Lord Robert Cecil and others were complaining at the punishment meted out to the Suffragette prisoners. Many Liberals found difficulty in reconciling themselves to the thought that Richard Cobden's daughter was being treated by a Liberal government as though she were a common criminal. It was therefore suddenly decided that the militant women prisoners should be accorded the status of first class misdemeanants. On being informed of her new status, Sylvia consulted the prison rules, and discovered that she was now entitled to exercise her profession, and claimed the right to send for drawing-paper, pen, ink, and pencils. After a day's waiting this was granted, and she began busily drawing prison scenes. The gaol, as she later recalled, thus "lost the worst of its terrors", as she had "congenial work to do".

Anxious to reveal the awful conditions of prison life, as well as to advance the women's cause, she held press interviews after her release on November 6, and was quoted by many newspapers as declaring that the thing which impressed her most was "the terrible isolation and loneliness and misplaced work". The prison, she said, operated "as if it were still in the Middle Ages."[5] To support what she said she provided the journalists with copies of her prison sketches.

Shortly after her release from prison Sylvia took a holiday – a rare event in her life, and one which was to become increasingly infrequent in ensuing years – travelling to Italy for a fortnight with Mrs. Pethick Lawrence and staying at Venice and Torcello. Sylvia's second visit to Italy was artistically notable, for after her imprisonment she revelled in the sunshine. While Mrs. Pethick Lawrence and her husband were still asleep, she would walk into the countryside and spend the day sketching men, women and children, stopping only on the coming of twilight. She was happy to return, if only briefly, to her life as an art student. It is impossible to identify which of her known works were in fact produced on this brief visit, for which reason, as already noted, all her Venice pictures have been described in Chapter 3.

Now keenly interested in prisons, it was not long before she went with Mrs. Pethick Lawrence to inspect the women's gaol in Milan. This institution, she said, seemed "bright and homely" after Holloway's "machine-like grimness". The cells were moreover roomy and the windows and furniture resembled those of an ordinary house, though the exercise ground with each prisoner in a separate little yard guarded by a soldier with a gun, appeared "a relic of earlier barbarism".[6]

Returning once more to London she resumed her artistic-cum-political life. She wrote an article on British and Italian prisons, which appeared in the *Pall Mall Magazine* with drawings (Nos. 13 and 14) based on her original sketches, which are no longer extant. She was also at about this time invited to produce a poster for the social reformer W. T. Stead, who was then contemplat-

Left: No. 13: Sketch of Italian prison exercise enclosure, redrawn by an engraver for the *Pall Mall Magazine*, January–June 1907.

Opposite: No. 14: Prison sketches from Holloway Prison, redrawn by an engraver for the *Pall Mall Magazine*, January–June 1907.

Ready for Supper

Scrubbing the Bed

Dinner

The Bread Basket

ing publishing a series of children's books in colour, and so she began a cartoon of Queen Boadicea riding into battle on a chariot.

The picture was still unfinished on February 12, 1907, when Parliament reassembled to hear the King's Speech which, as it turned out, made no mention of votes for women. The first "Women's Parliament"* met the following day in the Caxton hall. From there the participants, Sylvia included, formed up in orderly procession and made their way towards the House of Commons.

It was cold but a shimmering day, the sun a delicate rain – washed blue and the sunshine gleaming on the fine gilded pointing on the roof of the tall clock tower. We stepped out smartly and all seemed to be going well, but when those in front reached the green in front of the Abbey, a body of police barred their way and an inspector called them back, and ordered his men to break up the procession. The police strode through our ranks, but the women at once united again and pressed bravely on. A little further we went thus, when suddenly, a body of mounted police came riding up. In an instant Mrs. Despard and several others in the front rank were arrested, and the troopers were urging their horses into the midst of the women behind, scattering them right and left.

Still we strove to reach our destination, and returned again and again. Those of us who rushed from the roadway on to the pavement were pressed by the horses closer and closer against the walls and railings until at last we retreated or were forced away by the constables on foot. Those of us who took refuge in door-ways were dragged roughly down the steps and hurled back in front of the horses. When even this failed to banish us, the foot constables rushed at us, catching us fiercely by the shoulders, turned us round again and then seizing us by the back of the neck and thumping us cruelly between the shoulders forced us at a running pace along the streets until we were far from the House of Commons. They had been told to drive us away and to make as few arrests as possible. Still we returned again, until the last five women and two men, all of them bruised and dishevelled, had been taken to the police station, and those who had not been arrested were almost fainting from fatigue. Then, after ten o'clock, the police succeeded in clear-ing all the approaches to the House of Commons, and the mounted men were left galloping about in the empty square till midnight, when the House rose.[7]

Sylvia was among the fifty-four women and two men subsequently sentenced – in her case to three weeks' imprisonment. Her arrest having been in no way premeditated, she had made no plans for her detention. During her incarcera-tion she wondered if she had left her studio window open, if the rain had driven in, and whether the picture of Boadicea would be blown from the easel by the wind.

---

* In the course of the Suffragette movement ten such women's assemblies were held in the Caxton Hall, Westminster.

No. 15: Prison sketch of inmate of Holloway Prison, reproduced in *Votes for Women*, January 7, 1909.

Taking advantage of the freedom then allowed to Suffragette prisoners – it was later to be withdrawn – she once again busied herself drawing scenes of prison life, and collecting information to assist subsequent agitation for prison reform. One of the sketches (No. 15) made at this time, or on her previous imprisonment, is preserved in the files of the Suffragette journal *Votes for Women*: it is a simple pen and ink drawing of a woman wearing characteristic prison garb, with a bonnet bearing a broad arrow[8] – a symbol with which she was to become increasingly familiar in the years to come.

On her release she found her Boadicea unhurt, and completed the picture for Stead, but learned that it was unwanted as he had abandoned his plan for the series. He asked her instead to produce black-and-white drawings for his penny booklets. However, she was enraged when on leaving he seized her in his arms, and struggling to escape she fled from the building without a word.

Despite her two imprisonments, in the first months of 1907 she had still not abandoned her aspiration to devote her life to art. She received strong encouragement for this ambition from an Italian woman artist, Emilia Cemino Folliero, who attended the second "Women's Parliament" in March 1907 – and was arrested, almost unintentionally, together with seventy-five women and one man. She often called on Sylvia, and urged her to escape from the turmoil of the Suffragette movement, which she regarded as entirely inimical to artistic work, and pressed her to go with her to paint in an old castle in the Italian mountains. Sylvia was tempted, but refused.

7 Studying and Sketching Women's Work in Northern England and Scotland; Electioneering for the WSPU

IN THE EARLY SUMMER OF 1907 Sylvia decided to leave London, then awhirl with Suffragette activity, for the north, for places where women were grievously exploited in industry and agriculture, and where they were in many cases scarcely or not at all organised. Anxious to study the life of the working people, and to record significant details about their life, and the grim surroundings in which they dwelt, she packed her paints, together with a tiny case of clothes, some books and a small amount of money – and prepared herself, as earlier in Venice, for a spell of solitude and hard work. She travelled as an artist and writer intent on recording significant details about working people and sought to do so with sympathy, but without sentimentality, rhetoric, or invective.

The sketches and paintings of working women she now embarked upon had necessarily to be carried out at speed, and, being pressed for time, she turned to gouache. She had already used this medium in Italy and on the WSPU membership card, and seems to have found that it enabled her to capture likenesses in the short snatches of time which her sitters could spare, or which the situation allowed her. She tried to draw what she saw, without any attempt to produce works of beauty.

Her first visit was to the Black Country of Staffordshire where she established herself in Cradley Heath to investigate the conditions of the women employed in the making of chains and nails. The most they then earned was 5 shillings a week. She stayed as a paying guest with an old woman who ran a sweet shop and who was perhaps the subject of the gouache and watercolour full length portrait of an old woman in black (Plate IV).

Sylvia went out each day to paint pictures of the women working at the forges in the dilapidated workshops, and in the evening wrote accounts of what she observed. Unfortunately not one of her paintings of the women chain-makers has come to light, but it is possible, however, that the gouache and watercolour of a tumbledown and grimy red brick cottage with barred window openings next to a factory or mill buildings (Plate VII) may have been one she produced in the Black Country.

She was appalled by the grey desolation and utter neglect for human life which she saw there. Never had she seen "so hideous a disregard of elementary decencies in housing and sanitation as in that area. Roads were too often beaten tracks of litter-fouled earth; rubbish heaps often abounded; jerry-built hovels crumbled in decay. The country was utterly blighted; there were none of the usual amenities of town life, only its grosser ugliness."[1]

Recalling the conditions of the men and women workers who lived in this wasteland she later wrote:

> The men in the chain trade earned unusually high wages, but they had virtually no outlet save the public house.
>
> The women were working eight or ten hours a day at the domestic forge to earn a miserable four or five shillings a week, doing such domestic work as they could by the way. Their faces were drawn with toil, their garments flecked with small holes burnt by the flying sparks. Often a white-faced baby, scarcely taken out of the dark hovel from week to week, sat in a tiny chair beside the anvil, watching its mother's hammer; sometimes a child got a speck of red-hot coke in its face, but in general the sparks flew the other way. The women told me they worked thus to gain some money of their very own, but actually they were simply following the traditions of the district; all the women made chains as a matter of course. The women were the drudges of the industry; they made only the common "slap" chain, as it was called, for which speed was required but not great accuracy. The trade union prohibited them from the better work.

There were no recreations except perhaps an annual fair. The cinema had not yet reached those parts. There were no libraries, no public baths, only the most miserable shops. One had to walk far to find green country.

She was "wounded to see a mother, or sometimes an old grandmother, blowing the bellows at a paltry wage of a lad in his teens, already doing skilled work, and occupying an industrial status which his mother could never attain".[2]

She was on the point of leaving Cradley Heath with a bundle of pictures when she received a telegram from her mother summoning her to join her at Rutland where there was to be a by-election, for which the WSPU was short of speakers and needed Sylvia's services.

While working in the constituency she came across a further example of discrimination against women. In the days when voters were scarce before the

Reform Act of 1884 which had enfranchised agricultural labourers, widows and their daughters had frequently been turned out of their farms, not because they could not pay their rent, but because they were not entitled to vote, and were therefore of no electoral value to the landowner. Even at the time of her visit a woman tenant was still regarded with disfavour on that account.

Electioneering for the WSPU in Rutland was at times hard going as she and her comrades had to contend with the gangs of youths hired by some local tradesmen and gentry to "punish the Suffragettes". Most people attending the women's meetings nonetheless purchased pamphlets or badges, and the speakers were cheerily hailed from afar by workers labouring among the crops as well as by the drivers of passing carts. Men, women and children ran to cottage doors to see the visitors pass, and everywhere they were greeted by smiles and kindly words.[3]

After the election she went to Leicester where, renting a room, she proceeded to meet, study, draw, and rally the workers in the shoemaking industry. She made contact with a small producers' cooperative factory. The work struck her as most monotonous, but when the women stopped their toil after hours of some oft-repeated operation, such as machining toecaps, she was surprised that many of them, crowding round her easel, would exclaim, "I should never have the patience to do it!" She also held numerous meetings in Leicester for the WSPU.[4]

Her visit to Leicester resulted in an interesting gouache and watercolour portrayal of women workers in a shoe factory (Plate V). The painting gives a vivid impression of workshop conditions, with heads bent over the bench, and several of the women wear glasses. The composition is in pastel shades, the women in pale blue smocks, and the windows providing an element of luminosity.

Another work of this period is a drawing in red, black and white chalk on olive grey paper (Plate VI) of a girl seated beside a machine used in shoemaking. A label on the back reads: "skiving or thinning off the edges of the different parts of the shoe ready for fitters and machinists."

From Leicester she travelled to Wigan in Lancashire to see the "pit brow" girls who laboured in the local coal industry. She found that they wore "the usual Lancashire clogs, with bonnets upon their heads and shawls over their shoulders." They had short corduroy knickerbockers, over which they used to wear a blue print apron called a "coat" which had the advantage over an ordinary skirt in that should it catch in any of the machinery it was easy to unbutton and slip off, whereas, in the case of an ordinary skirt, "a woman would be unable to free herself, and would be drawn into the machinery and crushed." With the more adequate fencing of machinery "coats" were, however, beginning to disappear.

The term "pit brow lassies" included bankswomen, pit brow lassies proper, sorters and screenwomen. The bankswomen stood in pairs at the mouth of the shaft reaching down into the mine below. As the cage laden with coal-filled tubs came to the surface and then stopped these women entered it, and between them dragged the tubs out one by one, and with a hard push sent them rolling off along the railway lines. This work was sometimes done by men, sometimes by women, but though banksmen and bankswomen stood together at the shaft, and worked the same number of hours at the same task the women earned less than half as much as the men.

The tubs rolled off at the push of the banksmen and bankswomen and were met by a group of pit brow lassies, who pushed and dragged and guided them on their way to the sorting screens. In some cases a woman with a knowledge of coal was stationed at a point to which all the tubs had to come where the lines leading to the various screens diverged. According to the size and quality of the coal each tub contained, she decided in which direction it should go, turning the points for it and pushing it on towards the receiver into which it was emptied, and whence the coal fell into one of the sorting screens.

The latter were in the form of long belts which moved continuously and carried the coal with them. They were usually some three feet wide, and about three feet from the ground. On either side of the belts rows of women stood picking out pieces of stone, wood, and other waste stuff from amongst the coal as it slowly moved past. Sometimes they picked out pieces of waste with their fingers, and sometimes with a hammer they struck off those which might be adhering to the coal itself. Some collieries supplied plenty of tools for coal sorting but in others most of the work was done with the fingers. Serious accidents on the pit brow were by this time rare, but minor accidents to the fingers, caused frequently by large pieces of coal falling on them, were not uncommon. Moreover, the dust from the coal was constantly rising, and the women's faces, hands and clothing were soon blackened. Their heads were closely muffled in shawls to protect their hair. In some cases the belt was so arranged that it was necessary for two women to kneel on the ground at the end of it to attend to the aperture by which the coal passed off the belt, and to prevent it becoming clogged.

The sorting of coal entailed "practically no physical exertion" but the work of the bankswomen and pit brow lassies necessitated "great muscular strength and power of endurance," both of which they possessed "in abundant measure". Indeed, seeing them working side by side with the men, they appeared "almost stronger than the latter". Many were "splendidly made, lithe and graceful", and, including the sorters, for all the coal dust, had clear, fresh complexions. Their rosy cheeks contrasted strangely with the "wan white faces of their sisters in the neighbouring cotton mills."[5]

Sylvia, whose face was soon blackened like those of the pit brow girls, found them "hard and stout workers, genial and uncomplaining." Many of them, she discovered, preferred their work to that in factories; in the latter silence was usually enforced while there was "considerable freedom at the pit, and the lassies laugh and call to each other as they pull the tubs about."

Sorting, she felt, was, however, "a soul-destroying job which should be reduced, or, if possible, replaced by machinery." She was later to express surprise that some of her women's suffrage colleagues should praise it, and chain-making, as evidence of women's equality with men. Some women's groups, she complained, had organised deputations to argue that there should be no suppression of such work, but had done nothing to demand better pay and conditions, both of which were so urgently needed.[6]

Sylvia's stay in Wigan in the summer of 1907 coincided with a period of internal strife within the Suffragette movement. Her mother, with whom she corresponded during her spell of self-imposed isolation, faced with disputes over tactics, as well as conflicts of personality, wrote to her that she had decided to abolish the WSPU's elective constitution, and to make herself dictator with the right to appoint and dismiss the committee. Sylvia, a democrat, thought this move ill-judged, and wrote back: "Do not fear the democratic constitution. You can carry the conference with you. There is no doubt of it." She might, she later observed, "have as well urged the wind to cease from blowing!" The majority of the WSPU duly accepted Mrs. Pankhurst's policy – though a minority broke away to form a separate organisation, the Women's Freedom League.

Sylvia was still in Wigan when she was called by telegram to work for her mother at another by-election, this time in Bury St. Edmunds.

She seems at about this time to have returned to Staffordshire to visit the potteries where, gaining admission to one of the principal firms, she saw "haggard women scouring off the powdered flint dust from the newly baked unglazed ware", the biscuit, as it was called. The deadly dust, the women told her, injured the lungs of the workers who could be protected if only greater thought, and expenditure, were devoted to the matter.

She went into the dipping shed where the ware was glazed, and where she fainted twice on the first morning. All the time she was there she "continually felt a sensation of pressure and discomfort in the ears and throat, and a desire to swallow and draw saliva into the mouth, and had after a time the nasty sweet taste of which the lead workers complain". Struck by the "leaden pallor of the workers", she marvelled and grieved that in that magnificent establishment, as in most others, use was made of lead glaze. The men who plunged the pottery into it suffered from lead paralysis, or "waist drop" as they called it, while the women who scraped off surplus glaze contracted lead colic and jaundice. Their wombs often became infected and in many cases they gave birth to stillborn babies or ones that died of convulsion soon after birth. She was also horrified to learn that women working under these most dangerous conditions earned no more than seven shillings a week. When she asked whether the continued use of lead glaze was necessary she was told that it saved fuel as it could be used over a greater range of temperature than any other, and that private manufacturers could not be expected to spend money on research for purely humanitarian reasons. Moreover, they said, catalogues and price lists would have to be changed if new substances were to be employed. How, she exclaimed, could price lists and catalogues be weighed against the lives of human beings?

Wedgwood's factory provided a remarkable contrast from most other firms, for in the production of jasper and other fine wares no lead was used. Delighted at this she tried her hand at making some cups and saucers which she painted and I recall her on more than one occasion urging friends, where possible, to buy Wedgwood pottery.*

In the potteries, as elsewhere, she saw how women workers were subordinated to men. Women turned the wheels for men throwers, and trod the lathe for men turners. In each case the woman was employed by the man for whom she toiled – she was the slave of a slave, Sylvia thought. Here once again women were debarred from the better paid, more highly skilled jobs, in this case by arrangement between the employers and the unions.[7]

---

* A member of the Wedgwood family, the Labour MP Colonel Josiah Wedgwood, was, it is interesting to note, much later to give her staunch support in her agitation to preserve the independence of Ethiopia, and, at the close of the Second World War, to prevent the return to Italy of its former colonies.

No. 16: *In a Pot Bank: Scouring and Stamping the Maker's Name on the Biscuit China.*

No less than eight of her works in the potteries are extant. A charcoal drawing (No. 16) depicts four women hard at work, their heads covered against the dust which they were, however, inhaling. They are, as the title says, *In a Pot Bank. Scouring and Stamping the Maker's Name on the Biscuit China.* A gouache and watercolour (No. 17) is of a red-haired girl working in a pottery, the late afternoon light catching her hair and blouse. The caption at the back, now partly obscured, reads, " . . . in a Pot Bank. Scouring and dusting after the . . . has . . .". Another gouache and watercolour (No. 18) shows a plumpish woman working by the pottery window. A third, in the same media (No. 19) shows an "old fashioned pottery" in which a woman and a girl are "transferring the pattern onto the biscuit". A beautiful soup tureen shines in the foreground. A charcoal drawing (No. 21) reveals a girl at work, and bears the title: *In a Pot Bank. In the Dipping House. Scraping off the Superfluous Glaze.*

No. 17: Untitled. A red-headed girl working in a pottery.

Another charcoal drawing with a trace of gouache (No. 20), entitled *Dipping and Drying on the Mangle,* presents a girl and a stunted man, both standing. Blobs and smears of white gouache have been added to the foreground in an attempt to indicate spills and splashes of clay. A gouache and watercolour (No. 22) is of an apprentice "thrower" assisted by his young girl "baller". The last, and perhaps most striking of the pottery series, a gouache and watercolour (Plate VIII), is particularly detailed. It shows an elderly craftsman turning jasper ware in an old fashioned pottery, with, as usual, a woman assistant in attendance. The painting is in light shades, with a predominance of whites and greys which gives a luminous appearance.

Opposite: No. 18: *In a Pot Bank: Finishing off the Edges of the Unbaked Pots on a Whirler.*

No. 20: *Dipping and Drying on the Mangle.*

No. 21: *In a Pot Bank: in the Dipping House Scraping off the Superfluous Glaze.*

From the potteries she travelled to Scarborough to examine the conditions of the Scottish fisherwomen who moved along the east coast in the wake of the herrings. These women struck her as "beautified by their outdoor life", and they sang and chattered "like a shoal of sea birds" over the fish they cleaned and packed. She lodged with a fisherman's wife in the old town, "a jolly woman, with quaint stories, grave and merry."

> I wept when she told me of how the Scotch herring fleet, setting off to reach home by Christmas, had been caught by a squall and wrecked within sight of her windows, the toys the fishermen had brought for their children thrown up with their bodies on the shore. She made me laugh, in spite of myself, over her first adventure in domestic service as a child of fourteen. Her young master, before departing for his office each morning, would tell her that she must on no account permit her mistress to do any housework. The young mistress had usually no desire to offend in that direction, but one day confided her intention to make a cake. It was a cake of a very special kind, comprised entirely of eggs and butter, and so light that it must only be beaten by the tips of the fingers, which proved an exceedingly messy proceeding. Finally it was stowed in a hot oven for half an

Opposite: No. 19: *Old-Fashioned Pottery: Transferring the Pattern onto the Biscuit.*

No. 22: *On a Pot Bank: an Apprentice "Thrower" and his "Baller" at Work.*

No. 23: *Scotch Fisher Lassies. Two Old Folk Packing Herrings.*

hour. When the door was opened the poor mistress gave a cry of dismay, the servant burst into laughter. Next day she ran away to her mother, the milkman helping her with her box.[8]

Her sojourn at Scarborough led to the production of at least two gouache and watercolours, one (Plate IX) of a robust fisherwoman in an orange headscarf cutting herrings, with barrels in the background, and the other (No. 23) of two old women packing the fish into the barrels.

She went northwards next to the border counties and rented a room in the autumn from a widow at Churnside in Berwickshire. There she studied the work of the women agricultural labourers and painted these neat, quaintly dressed and well-spoken farmhands.

Fascinated by their "old world peasant costume", and intent on catching every detail of it for her sketches, she notes that these women wore "big black hats with great wide brims" and underneath them:

> … pink cotton handkerchiefs, worn over the head, drawn closely around the face, and pinned together under the chin and on the breast. These handkerchiefs are all of one pattern, a small red and white check that appears pink at a distance, with a ruching of red on red and white scalloped cotton or woollen stuff: the brim is sometimes left plain, but generally has a white or pink gathered lining, finished off at the end with a red or black ruche about an inch in width. The women are also wearing short petticoats of brown or grey woollen stuff striped with tiny lines of red, blue or other colours, and have aprons of similar material. Their bodices, plainly made and buttoned in front, are of various colours, but most frequently blue or red.

In cold weather the women she saw and painted often wore little plaid shawls and black knitted armlets to keep them warm, but when it was damp and chilly they put on big thick jackets and leather leggings.

Seeing several little groups of women among sheaves of corn stalks she sought to investigate, and doubtless also sketch, their work which she described in faithful detail. She found that they were "stooking", or setting up the sheaves which had been left lying on the ground by the reapers (who were men). Each "stook" consisted of eight sheaves, three pairs facing each other and one at each end.

Holding a sheaf in either arm two women met and propped the four sheaves together. Another woman meanwhile added a third pair, while a fourth woman placed a single sheaf at either end of the group thus made. Four other women were at the same time making "stooks" of adjoining sheaves, so that eight women thus crossed the field in two zigzag lines, "stooking" all the way, until they had covered the whole field and there were no more sheaves left lying on the ground.

The women, she was interested to note, while working were gentle in their movements, and were not silent, but spoke softly, thus, she fancied, seeming to catch something of the spirit of the birds and little mice that also lived amongst the corn.

She was also interested to watch the workers "leading", that is to say gathering the corn together and building it up into stacks. Far off, across the field, men and women were forking the sheaves of corn up on to the carts, and, when these were fully laden, she saw them driven towards her, some by women in brightly coloured clothing, others by men in sober brown and grey.

As they came toiling up the hill the big farm horses panted and snorted under their load. At last – some quietly, others twisting and plunging amid cries of "Whoa! Back man! Back! Back woman!" from the drivers – the horses reached the stacks and drew up the carts behind them.

Then followed the work of loading – which was the subject of one of her pictures. Seeking to record the toil as truthfully as she knew how she writes:

> The first stack has already grown high and the woman driver standing up on a wooden bar fastened across the top of the cart has to fork the sheaves far up across her head. High up on the stack a girl catches them as they come swinging through the air and throws them from her to a man, who crawls kneeling and placing the sheaves carefully round the top of the stack – the heads of grain turned inward and the stalks touching the outer edge – and then stands up and throws the sheaves down on the stack as he catches them to form an inner circle. Layer after layer of sheaves is laid down in this way and soon the straight up walls of the stack are finished and then the circular layers grow smaller and smaller to form the pointed roof. So small are they grown at last that but a few sheaves suffice to form one of the circles, and the man gets round the top of the stack in a moment. So high is the stack now that the girl who catches the sheaves has to bend far forward to reach them, though the woman in the cart, raising both arms above her head and holding the fork at its extremest end, tosses the corn up as far as ever she can.
>
> At last the point of the stack is reached and the girl, standing upon the slope and clinging to it with one arm and hand, passes the last sheaves to the man, who lays them on the sloping roof and ties the tops together with a rope of straw, then rakes and pats the whole stack over to make its surface regular and smooth.
>
> Meanwhile all the farmhands are busy in the same way, working their hardest to build up a row of stacks each from its first straw foundation to the pointed top.

Work stopped between three and four o'clock, when the men, women, boys and girls sat down for tea. This was brought out to the field in neat little bags, one for each worker, tied with a drawing tape, and containing a tin bottle of tea and either homemade scones, bread and butter, or bread and jam. Each of these bags was packed in the worker's own house, and the print of which it was made was of a different colour or pattern from every other, and could thus be easily identified.

On wet days the workers were generally to be found in the barns, where Sylvia drew them making straw ropes for thatching stacks, threshing corn, and bruising oats. In a description of the backbreaking labour which she was also to portray in watercolour, she recalls that two women wearing pink handkerchiefs and small cloth caps upon their heads would be feeding the bruiser.

One woman scoops up some of the oats that are lying in heaps upon the granary floor and pours them into a sack, which is held open by her companion, who afterwards helps her to hoist the full sack on her back. As the first woman carries the heavy sack away and with it mounts the steps leading to an upper chamber, from which she can pour the oats down into the "bruiser", the second woman is beginning to fill another sack. When the first woman comes down again she will hold the mouth of the sack open and help the second one to lift it on to her back, just as was done in her own case. So, each one doing her part in turn, the work goes on.

In the adjoining barn the oats come down from the upper chamber into the lower part of the bruiser, which discharges the grain into a sack ready to receive it. Two or three women will be working here – hooking the empty sack in position, putting a fresh one in its place when it is filled, and carrying the sacks full of bruised oats away on their shoulders to be stored in the granary at the other end of the yard.

In the loft where the woman pours the oats into the top of the bruiser, the upper part of the threshing machine is also situated. A cart laden with corn has been drawn close up in the yard outside and a man, or woman, as the case may be, is standing upon it and forking the sheaves in through a narrow opening on to a moving belt which carries them to the threshing machine. In the dim loft the out-side light streams through the opening and falls upon the corn sheaves making them seem wonderfully warm and golden as they come sliding in.

A girl standing on the top of the threshing machine cuts the straw band from each sheaf as it comes in and then passes the corn on to a middle-aged man – her father, as it happens – who opens out the sheaves and lets them be carried down with a rush into the lower part of the machine. Meanwhile there is a rattling noise like the falling of hailstones and we know that the ripe grain is being beaten from the ears. There is a feeling of bustle and excitement and the whole building throbs with the vibration of the machine. Down below on the ground floor, masses of yellow straw is pouring constantly out and the women are hurrying away with great piles of it bigger than themselves.

Work was done in this manner in Northumberland, Durham and the border counties of Scotland where there were large farms employing from twenty to thirty labourers, half or even more of whom were frequently women. It was customary for a farmer to hire a man with his family, though a woman, usually a widow, might sometimes be employed with several of her sisters. The work-ing hours for men and women, she discovered, were the same, but the latter received lower wages, and were once more at a serious disadvantage, for whereas "the men receive their wages regularly during the whole time of their engagement, even when absent through illness, holidays, or other causes, the women, if they are absent through illness or other personal reasons, or if the weather happens to be too stormy for them to work, or the farmer has no work for them to do, are not paid."[9]

Sylvia also saw something of the casual women potato pickers who came from the slums of Berwick-on-Tweed. Their work was geared to that of a ploughman whose horses pulled a plough through a field full of the withered stalks of potato plants, thus leaving an open furrow where the tubers could be seen lying amid the moist dank earth. Following in the wake of the plough was "a long line of women stooping and bending, bending and stooping, over the furrows, groping with their hands in the loose soil, and gathering up the potatoes as they came". There were also three or four men in the field who, significantly enough, were "overlookers and ... stood talking and smoking by the hedge, and from time to time carried away the filled potato baskets that the women had placed ready, and emptied them into the potato 'pit'. Hour after hour the women went on toiling with bent backs and eyes fixed to the ground, until at last one of the men shouted to them to stop, for it was half-past twelve."

Then the potato pickers rose, straightened themselves, and left the field, thus giving the artist her first clear sight of them. They were, she exclaimed:

> ... poor, miserable creatures, clad in vile, nameless rags, sometimes pinned, some-
> times tied round them with other rags or bits of string. They were old women
> with their skin all gnarled and wrinkled, and their purple lips all cracked. There
> were young women with dull white sullen faces, many with scars or black bruises
> round the eyes, and swollen, shapeless lips. Their hair was all matted and neg-
> lected, and every woman's eyes were fiery red.
>
> They came and squatted on the piles of straw laid ready for covering the
> potatoes, and began each one to eat her meal of bread and jam or bread and
> cheese, or dry bread alone. As they did so they shouted to each other, in loud
> harsh voices, coarse, ribald jokes and oaths, and then laughed at them with awful
> laughter. When they had finished eating, the elder women sat talking more quietly,
> and smoking short clay pipes, whilst the younger women either lay about half-
> asleep in the straw or chased each other across the field with rough horseplay.
>
> At one o'clock the men called them back to their work again, and so they
> went on till five, when they gathered together their ragged shawls and outer
> garments, and noisily left the field.
>
> Beside the three straw-covered lorries on which they were driven back to their
> homes in Berwick-on-Tweed, I saw them standing huddled together, these poor,
> degraded creatures lower than the beasts of the field.[10]

PLATE IV Untitled. Full-length portrait of old woman.

Opposite: PLATE V Untitled. Women working at benches in a shoemaking factory.

PLATE VI **In a Leicester Boot Factory: "Skiving" or Thinning off the Edges of the Different Parts of the Shoe Ready for the Fitters and Machinists.**

PLATE VII Untitled. Dilapidated red-brick cottage.

These women, it transpired, worked for contractors under rough gangsmen, and while the potatoes were being sorted and piled in the "pit" she heard their stories, "sordid and grey, with the workhouse as the inevitable harbour of old age". The women seemed so terrible, sitting silently by her easel, that she could scarcely force herself to stay with them. Poor humanity ! she cried.[11]

Painting these and other agricultural workers presented difficulties as the women were constantly on the move, and she could only catch brief glimpses of any particular subject. Recalling one of her sketches* – of a little girl with the black hat and traditional blue blouse and red ruche of the Berwickshire farm women – she later recalled: "It was a pity I could not finish it but I never saw the girl again after she consented to stand in the field a little while, and also I had a telegram from my mother to go somewhere else so I packed up and left."[12]

Three gouache and watercolours date from her stay in Berwickshire. The first (Plate x) depicts two women farm labourers loading produce on the back of a horse-drawn cart. A second is of a group of men and one woman in a shed, some of them in the background, making straw ropes. The third (Plate xi, which was later to be reproduced in *Votes for Women*) perhaps in the loft of the same building, shows a man and a woman working at the top of an elevator, and is entitled, *Berwickshire Farm Hands Threshing*.

As winter set in she moved to Glasgow where her beloved brother Harry, then a stripling of eighteen, was working for a local builder. Though glad of Harry's company at weekends, she did not live with him but obtained a lodging in a two-roomed flat in a tenement building in Bridgton. She occupied the parlour, and slept in a bed-cupboard in the wall, the kindly master and mistress of the house moving with their adopted daughter into the kitchen. She obtained permission to paint in a nearby cotton mill. She began her work in the spinning-room which was so hot that she fainted almost at once, thus gaining permission to have a small window open beside her. In the interests of keeping the thread damp the operatives had of course to labour day in day out without any such privilege. They told her that "they were all made sick by the heat and bad air when they first began to work in the mills." The ring-spinning room where the little half-timers were employed was, she discovered, the worst of all.

*This sketch, which has a grey sky behind, cannot unfortunately be reproduced. Soon after her arrival in Ethiopia in 1956, my mother presented it to Emperor Haile Selassie's daughter Princess Tenagne Work and, as a result of the Ethiopian revolution of 1974, it has proved impossible to obtain a photograph of it in time for publication.

She found it impossible to work and grieved at the poor stunted children she saw there. It was, she felt, "a sight to make one rebel indeed !"

Painting in the mill throughout the day she devoted many of her evenings to speaking on women's suffrage or writing about the conditions of the factory operatives. Saturdays and Sundays she spent largely with Harry.[13]
Two scenes remain from her stay in the Glasgow cotton mills, both of them again in gouache and watercolour: in the first (No. 24) a barefooted woman is changing the bobbin, and in the second (Plate XII) another woman is "minding a pair of fine frames". Both women have sad, hopeless expressions, and look prematurely old.

Having completed her tour of the north, Sylvia returned to London, where she made a sketch, on Christmas Day 1907, of one of the leading Suffragettes, Mary Gawthorpe, whom she describes as "a winsome, merry little creature, with bright hair and laughing hazel eyes, a face fresh and sweet as a flower".[14] No trace of this work has, however, been found.

No. 24: *In a Glasgow Cotton Spinning Mill: Changing the Bobbin.*

8 Increased Suffragette Militancy; WSPU Designs and Banners; Decorations for the Prince's Skating Rink

DURING SYLVIA'S TOUR OF THE NORTH the women's movement had become increasingly militant. Within only a year or so of Annie Kenney's arrival to "rouse London", cabinet ministers had been obliged to cease addressing open meetings, and Liberal organisers were beginning to exclude women from their meetings. The number of Suffragette imprisonments greatly increased, from a total of 191 weeks in 1906–7 to 350 weeks in 1907–8, and the Government, adopting a more vindictive attitude, no longer accorded women political prisoners the status of first class misdemeanants.

When she returned from the north Sylvia once more became involved in WSPU activities in London. Because of her residence at Park Walk she served as unpaid organiser for Chelsea, Fulham and Wandsworth. In these areas she held a succession of meetings in open air pitches where no women's suffrage meetings had ever previously been held. Her experience was invariably the same. "Our first meeting", she says, "was, usually, almost wholly a fight to subdue a continued uproar. On more than one occasion the little box or chair used as a platform was overturned by a gang of hooligan youths, and the meeting had to be abandoned. But, whatever may have happened at the first meeting in a fresh place, we always found that at the second meeting the majority of the audience was sympathetic. At the third meeting all was harmony, and we were generally seen to our homeward trains or buses by cheering crowds."[1]

The growth of popular support for women's enfranchisement became apparent in June 1908 when in response to it the old National Union of Women's Suffrage Societies called a great Albert Hall meeting which was joined by numerous organisations, including the women of the Independent Labour Party, women's Liberal Associations, the Fabian Society, and many other groups. Sylvia, looking at the event as an artist as well as a Suffragette, described it as "a striking pageant with its many gorgeous banners, richly embroidered and fashioned of velvets, silks and every kind of beautiful material and the small bannerettes serving as innumerable patches of brilliant and lovely colour, each one varying both in shape and hue." Several were blazoned with the figures of great women in history, among them Joan of Arc, Queen Elizabeth I, the penal reformer Elizabeth Fry, and the early women suffragists, Mary Wollstonecraft and Lydia Becker. "The procession", she said, "was acknowledged to be the most picturesque and effective political pageant that had ever been seen in this country."[2]

The WSPU meanwhile had been organising its own rally which took place on June 21. For it Sylvia prepared various heraldic designs and border decorations which were given to a firm specialising in the manufacture of banners, bunting and other regalia. She had to do her part of the work in such haste, she affirmed, that "no great artistry" was involved in the work which was "mass production, in double-quick time". She nevertheless consoled herself with the thought that "so vast was the demonstration that the appearance of an individual banner counted for little," but it was "true to say that the creation of a Michael Angelo would have ranked low in the eyes of WSPU enthusiasts beside a term served in Holloway goal".[3]

The demonstration drew vast crowds. "All London," she was afterwards to write, "seemed to have turned out to see us." Chelsea Embankment was thronged with people, and there were coffee stands, with costermongers, and and hawkers selling badges and programmes in the then newly devised Suffragette colours, purple, white and green. It was, she believed, "the greatest meeting that had ever been held", and the *Daily Chronicle* agreed: "Never, on the admission of the most experienced observers, has so vast a throng gathered in London to witness an outlay of political force."[4]

Having shown their ability to rally the general public the Suffragettes called a meeting shortly afterwards, on June 30, in Parliament Square. Though warned by the commissioner of police not to go to it, over a hundred thousand people are said to have made their way to Westminster where they were, however, prevented from assembling by a massed force of over five thousand police constables supported by upwards of fifty mounted men.

Suffragette activity was further intensified on the occasion of the state opening of Parliament on October 13. The WSPU distributed handbills far and wide calling men and women to "help the Suffragettes to rush the House of Commons". When the day came a kite bearing the words "Votes for Women" was raised over the Parliament building, while a steam launch covered with Suffragette posters patrolled the River Thames. Large numbers of men and women responded to the call to "rush" the House of Commons, and in the ensuing fracas twenty-four women and twelve men were taken to prison, and ten to hospital.

The following day Mrs. Pankhurst, Christabel and Flora Drummond were prosecuted for the handbill, and succeeded in having two members of the cabinet, Lloyd George and Herbert Gladstone, subpoenaed as witnesses, thus turning the court, for two whole days, into a Suffragette meeting.

Christabel on that occasion conducted a masterly, and long to be remembered, cross-examination which impressed all observers, not least her younger sister, who, with her constant eye for detail, describes her as dressed in a "fresh white muslin dress whose one note of colour was the broad band of purple, white and green stripes round her waist". Her soft brown hair was "uncovered, the little silky curls with just a hint of gold in them clustering about her neck ... her skin looking even more brilliantly white and those rose petal cheeks of hers even more exquisitely and vividly flushed with purest pink than usual.... She was as bright and dainty as a newly opened flower, and with all her look of perfect health and vigour, appeared so slender and so delicately knit as to have little more of substance in her than a briar rose." Christabel, she says, triumphed, however, "not by her grace and freshness", but by her "sparkling wit, her biting sarcasm and by the force and depth of her arguments" which were "enhanced by the everchanging eloquence of gesture, voice, and facial expression – by a lift of the eyebrows, a turn of the head, a heightening of the lovely rose colour that flooded sometimes as far as the white throat and as quickly ebbed again, a sweep of the slender hand or a turn of that slight virile frame. All these, because they so perfectly echoed and expressed her thoughts, could lend to even the baldest and tritest words, a forceful humour, a delicate irony, or an inexorable force."[5]

Despite her able defence Christabel was sentenced to ten weeks' imprisonment, and her mother and Mrs. Drummond to three months. During their enforced absence Sylvia was instructed by Mrs. Pethick Lawrence to take over the WSPU office once more, and dutifully abandoned all other activity. Learning that the prisoners were being punished for attempting to talk among themselves, she organised two successive processions to Holloway Prison. She and her comrades were greeted along the way by dense cheering crowds, but were prevented from reaching the prison by a force of police a thousand strong, so that she "doubted whether our voices, loud and numerous as they were, could be heard by the prisoners inside".[6]

Popular support was, however, sometimes offset by the efforts of

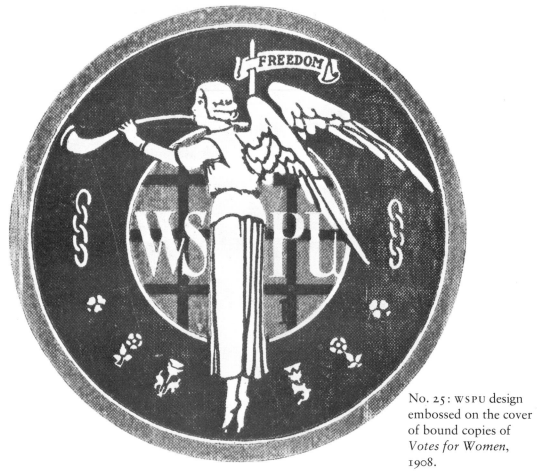

No. 25: WSPU design
embossed on the cover
of bound copies of
Votes for Women,
1908.

opponents to disrupt WSPU meetings. At a gathering at Ipswich, for example, she found that some prominent Liberals had paid men to create a disturbance, and as soon as she rose to speak she was assailed by shouts and yells while several fights broke out. Walking sticks were sent flying through the air and the smell of sulphurated hydrogen filled the hall.

While addressing and, in the absence of her mother and sister, organising numerous women's suffrage meetings she was also preparing heraldic emblems, Christmas cards and badges,* banners, illuminated addresses and other decorations for the growing movement for which she was now virtually the official artist. For some of these she charged a modest sum, but others she contributed

---

* The Suffragette journal, *Votes for Women,* announced, for example, on December 10, 1908 that a penny Christmas card with a "pretty design" by Sylvia Pankhurst was on sale, and on October 8, 1909 that a new coloured button bearing a "special design" by her in the movement's colours was then available. Price one penny.

No. 26: Suffragette tea service showing Sylvia's design of the angel.
PHOTO: MUSEUM OF LONDON

to the cause free of charge.[7]

Perhaps the earliest of these designs, conceived in 1908, was of a female angel, inspired perhaps by those she had seen depicted in Venice. This angel was standing tiptoe, blowing on a curved trumpet. Two versions of this device were produced. The first used had the angel facing left, apparently holding the instrument with only one arm. She carries behind her a small banner inscribed with the word "Freedom". In the background are prison bars and the letters "WSPU", with an encircling decoration of flowers, leaves and chains. This version of the drawing (No. 25) was embossed on the cover of bound copies of the weekly journal *Votes for Women*, edited by Mr. and Mrs. Pethick Lawrence, which were sold to supporters in annual volumes from October 1908.[8] (The publication also carried a long series of articles by the artist on the history of the women's movement.) The same design found its way on to a Suffragette tea service (No. 26), and, with the prison bars and surrounding chains and flowers omitted, appeared on at least one banner, that of the West Ham branch of the WSPU (No. 27). A work of distinction, preserved in the

No. 27: Banner of the West Ham branch of the WSPU.

Museum of London, it is of grey-green glazed cotton overlaid with purple and green velvet, with the words "Freedom" and "Courage Constancy Success" in white silk. A simpler version of the emblem (No. 28) with the angel facing to the right and holding the trumpet with two hands, but devoid of any background illustration, was subsequently used in the programme for the WSPU's Women's Exhibition in the Prince's Skating Rink of 1909 (see below).

Another device (Nos. 29 and 30), designed in 1908, is of a young girl in flowing robes striding forward through prison gates over broken chains. She brandishes a swirling ribbon-like banner bearing the slogan "Votes for Women". This insignia, used *inter alia* for a Christmas card issued by the National Women's Social and Political Union in 1908, was made into a Suffragette badge, and was later reproduced on the cover of Constance Lytton's *Prisons and Prisoners*, published in 1914.

Perhaps an even better known design (No. 31) was of a maiden sowing seeds, with the words "Votes for Women" above it, and beneath it, "Women's Social and Political Union". This emblem appeared on numerous WSPU

The National Women's Social & Political Union

4, Clement's Inn, London.

The Women's Exhibition 1909

Prince's Skating Rink Knightsbridge London

May 13th to 26th

Programme
Price 3D

The Woman's Press,
4, Clement's Inn, London, W.C.

N.W.S.P.U

VOTES
FOR
WOMEN

WITH BEST WISHES
FOR XMAS AND
THE NEW YEAR
1908 ⟶ 1909

"Strong Souls
Live like fire-hearted suns to spend
their strength"

Below: No. 30: Insignia reproduced
on the cover of Constance Lytton's
Prisons and Prisoners (London, 1914).

TO
GREET YOU

"What men call luck ⟶
Is the prerogative of valiant souls,
The fealty life pays its rightful kings."
James Russell Lowell.

Above: No. 31: Greetings card showing the sower.

Opposite: No. 28: Programme for the Women's Exhibition
in the Prince's Skating Rink, May 1909.

VOTES FOR WOMEN

EDITED BY FREDERICK AND EMMELINE PETHICK LAWRENCE.

VOL. IV. (New Series), No. 175. FRIDAY, JULY 14, 1911. Price 1d. Weekly (Post Free 1½d.)

THE COMING TOTAL ECLIPSE OF THE ANTI-SUFFRAGISTS.

"It is the duty of the National League for Opposing Woman Suffrage to stir up people from their apathy . . . there is very great risk that the Conciliation Bill will be rushed through Parliament . . ."
—LORD CROMER.

Contemporary cartoon by "A Patriot", 1911.

handbills including one advertising a "mass meeting of women" at the Albert Hall on April 29, 1909, and was also printed on greetings cards. A redrawn figure of the sower later formed the central decoration of the skating rink decorations. The motif was subsequently taken up by an anonymous cartoonist, "A Patriot", in a contemporary cartoon of 1912.

Yet another design (No. 32) appeared on the WSPU's calendar for 1910. The central theme is once more of a winged female angel; she is holding a lamp and guiding, through hilly country by night, a woman in prison garb stamped

Opposite: No. 32: WSPU calendar, 1910.

PHOTO: INTERNATIONAL INSTITUTE OF SOCIAL HISTORY

A VOTES FOR WOMEN CALENDAR 1910.

W · S

P · U.

FREEDOM

To Elsa Gue.

On behalf of all women who will win freedom by the bondage which you have endured for their sake, and dignity by the humiliation which you have gladly suffered for the uplifting of our sex, We, the Members of the Women's Social and Political Union, herewith express our deep sense of admiration for your courage in enduring a long period of privation and solitary confinement in prison for the Votes for Women' Cause, also our thanks to you for the great service that you have thereby rendered to the Woman's Movement. Inspired by your passion for freedom and right may we and the women who come after us be ever ready to follow your example of self-forgetfulness and self-conquest, ever ready to obey the call of duty and to answer to the appeal of the oppressed.

Signed on behalf of the Women's Social and Political Union.

with the broad arrow bearing a standard. The rest of the calendar is covered with an intricate pattern of leaves and grapes and bears the initials "WSPU".

Besides these emblems she devised a number of WSPU banners, few of which, however, have survived. One of her favourites was a representation of a mother and worker, which was unveiled at the Portman Rooms, Baker Street, in 1908. A cartoon version of this design was placed over the WSPU literature stall at the Hungarian Exhibition at Earls Court in the same year.

Another four of her banners were unfurled at an impressive WSPU ceremony in the Queen's Hall on May 25. The first to be shown was that of the Bradford Union, which bore the city of Bradford's arms, and the motto, "Grant to womanhood the justice England should be proud to give." The second banner, which was particularly resplendent, with gold lettering surrounded by entwined wreaths of flowers and a deep border of violet on a green ground, bore the words, "Human Emancipation must precede Social Regeneration." The third banner, also with gold on green with a violet border, depicted a pelican – the symbol of sacrifice – piercing her breast to feed her young with her own blood, and the words, "Great souls live, like fire-heated suns, to spend their strength". The fourth and last of these banners bore a gold legend on violet, with the most provocative of legends: "Rebellion to tyrants is obedience to God".[9]

With the growth of militancy, and the resultant arrest of increasing numbers of women, the WSPU decided to present an illuminated address and a badge of honour to every one of its members who had suffered imprisonment for the cause. The address (No. 33), which bore the signature of Mrs. Pankhurst, was first handed, amid scenes of the greatest enthusiasm, to five

Right: No. 34: The Holloway Brooch.

Opposite: No. 33: Illuminated address, signed by Mrs. Pankhurst, first presented to five women releasees in September 1908. The artist's original design was much distorted in the lithographic reproduction.
PHOTO: MUSEUM OF LONDON

women releasees at a ceremony in the Portman Rooms, Baker Street, on September 1908 – and was later to be given to many other women who followed their proud example. The motif, which was circular, showed a woman displaying a banner bearing the word "Freedom", with a winged female angel holding a trumpet on either side, and a rainbow in the background. The decoration was executed, Sylvia later recalled, "at short notice, but with considerable care". It was, however, reproduced by lithography, and "in the re-drawing by a workman on the stone became almost unrecognisable", and caused her "youthful zeal much distress".[10]

The text, which was surrounded with a decoration of roses – one of her favourite floral motifs – read:

> On behalf of all women who will win freedom from bondage which you have endured for their sake, and dignity by the humiliation which you have gladly suffered for the uplifting of our sex, we, the members of the Women's Social and Political Union, herewith express our deep sense of admiration for your courage in enduring a long period of privation and solitary confinement in prison for the "Votes for Women" cause, also our thanks to you for the service that you have thereby rendered to the women's movement. Inspired by your passion for freedom and right, may we, and the women who come after us, be ever ready to follow your example of self-forgetfulness and self-conquest, ever ready to obey the call of duty and to answer to the appeal of the needy and the oppressed.[11]

One of the first five women to receive this document was Maud Joachim, niece of the famous violinist, and a gaunt, dedicated spinster, who, as I recall, was to help my mother long afterwards in the anti-Fascist, pro-Ethiopian cause. Another Suffragette Elsa Gye, whose address is preserved in the Museum of London, received it in April 1909, after six weeks' imprisonment for the then very typical offence of attempting to petition the Prime Minister.

The badge or medal of honour (No. 34), sometimes also referred to as the "Holloway brooch"*, was conceived in relatively simple terms. It consisted of a broad arrow in the Suffragette colours, purple, white and green, with silver chains on either side, and between them a portcullis with five tooth-like projections at the base.[12] The medallion acquired some fame in July when the home secretary Herbert Gladstone, seeking to justify the harsh treatment meted out to Suffragette prisoners, alleged that they had kicked and bitten their wardresses. The prisoners indignantly denied the allegation, whereupon the

---

* The design of this brooch, described in *Votes for Women* on April 16, 1909, was later used on the cover of the *Roll of Honour of Suffragette Prisoners 1905–1914*.

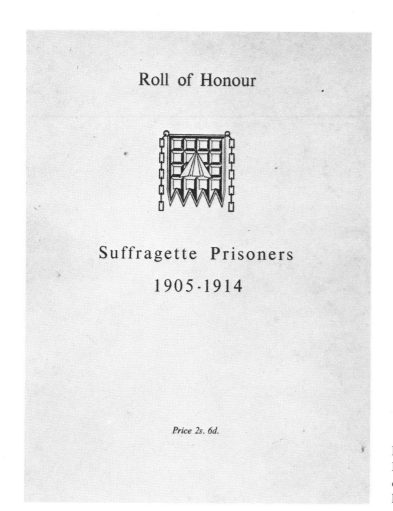

Roll of Honour

Suffragette Prisoners

1905-1914

Price 2s. 6d.

Design of the Holloway Brooch depicted on the *Roll of Honour* of Suffragette Prisoners, 1905–14.

minister replied that he had directed proceedings to be taken out against two women. Only one of them, as it turned out, was accused of biting. She was Miss Theresa Garnett* who claimed in her defence that the wound on the wardress's hand had been caused not by biting, but by the points of the portcullis. The case against her was dismissed, though Herbert Gladstone did not retract his statement.[13]

Though proud to have so fully contributed her artistic skill to the women's movement my mother was well aware of the limitations of some of her designs, the more so as "the urge for quantity, speed and some sort of economy inevitably worked many a transformation."[14]

---

* A portrait of Theresa Garnett wearing the portcullis badge is preserved in the Museum of London.

Left to Right: Emily Wilding Davison, Sylvia Pankhurst, displaying a wooden model of her Holloway Prison emblem, Christabel Pankhurst and Emmeline Pethick Lawrence in a Suffragette procession, 1910. PHOTO: DAVID MITCHELL

The WSPU decorations from which she drew the greatest artistic satisfaction were undoubtedly those she prepared for the great Women's Exhibition held in the Prince's Skating Rink, Knightsbridge, in May 1909. This work, which was requested by Mrs. Pethick Lawrence early in 1909, involved the design and execution of mammoth creations on canvas for a huge hall measuring two hundred and fifty feet by one hundred and fifty feet. Sylvia was given only three months to execute the project.

Her main problem was that the entire work had to be prepared outside the building, which could be hired only for the period of the exhibition, and then put up in the last few hours to cover the existing decorations and thus transform the whole place. The first three weeks she spent tramping, and travelling by bus – she had no access to a car – all round London in search of premises large enough to hold the designs which had to be no less than twenty feet high. Eventually she found a tall narrow chamber in the Avenue Studios in Fulham Road where the cartoons could be made, and a vast but not very lofty room over a nearby stable where other work could be carried out on the floor. So as "not to exploit the movement", she arranged for Amy Browning and two other women who had studied with her at the Royal College of Art to assist her for thirty shillings a week, the same modest wage as she allocated herself. Four former men students of the college also agreed to serve, for the then normal pay of a decorator – ten pence an hour.

The character of the designs and the whole scheme was conditioned, as she was later to explain, by "the necessity of doing something which could be executed in two months and one week precisely".

Planning the whole decoration herself, she made all the original designs which were a quarter of the final size, and painted them fully as they were to be reproduced. Because of the shortage of time she decided to paint by hand only the central paintings at each end of the hall, and to use stencils for the remainder of the decorations.

The men began the work by laying a pale cream colour on all the canvases, together measuring four hundred feet by twenty feet. Two of the women students in the Fulham Road studio meanwhile were enlarging the drawings for the arches and pilasters and four trees, one for each of the side panels at each end of the hall, as well as other decorations for the side walls. These enlargements were drawn in black on large sheets of white paper. As each black design was completed it was sent to the workshop where the men cut out the black to form stencil plates. For this purpose she borrowed a large table, and purchased pieces of glass for the men to cut on.

When the plates were completed, the men stencilled the designs on the canvases, copying her colours exactly for, as she recalled, "they were artists, not mere workmen". Meanwhile in the studio she was busy, with Amy Browning's help, enlarging and painting the figures.

All eight artists were thrilled by their first experience of having to accomplish a work of this magnitude, but nevertheless they faced many difficulties. To reach the higher parts of the decorations the women, in the studio, had to spend much of the time on ladder towers, while the men, in the stable, had to kneel on mats as they worked.

Shortage of space in which to work on such large canvases created many other problems, for, as she was to write many years later:

> The studio did not reach twenty feet in height and we were handicapped by the
> lack of width to step far back and survey the tall figures each about thirteen feet
> high. The studio did not allow the whole canvas to be extended a hundred and
> fifty feet. However, we rolled up the sides leaving open the portion to be painted.
> We could not get the whole height, so part of the top had to flop over and part of

the bottom had to lie on the floor. We had ladder towers which I hired to enable us to paint the upper part. The haste and the lack of space made the work difficult and consequently the enlargements did not equal the originals in certain particulars.[15]

The decorations, which were full of symbolism, not least in their frequent use of the Suffragette colours, purple, white and green, had for their theme the words of the Psalms. "They that sow in tears shall reap in joy. He that goeth forth and weepeth, bearing precious seed, shall doubtless come again with rejoicing, bringing his sheaves with him".

At the entrance were three arches and pilasters stencilled to represent ivy leaves. The central arch was decorated with ordinary ground ivy, while the side arches represented the more luxuriant tree ivy.

The central piece (No. 38), over the entrance, was a colossal figure of a woman – a redrawing of her sower (Plate XIII) – over thirteen feet high, sowing grain, with a flight of three doves overhead bearing an olive branch. She stands on a green sward, and around her feet spring daisies, daffodils, and many brightly-coloured wild flowers, while a briar rose in blossom rises up in a pattern-like quietness. Thistles in the background symbolise adversity. The woman appears eager and anxious, stepping forward and looking into an

35

36

unknown future. On either side of her are a small and a large arched panel, each containing representations of blossoming almond trees, before the appearance of their leaves, with crocuses at the foot of the trees, representing the first and fairest promise of spring.

Opposite, at the far end of the hall, was a joyous scene (No. 39). A woman clad in robes of neutral tint, relieved with purple whenever the robe is raised or drawn back, and radiant with triumph, bears a sheath of gathered grain. On either side of her, playing stringed instruments, stand bright-winged female angels on tiptoe. Above shines the sun, and beneath there is a green lawn with a garden of flowers in the centre. The design was set in a great arch formed of stylised trees, vines and ivy and bramble roses, laden with fruit and flowers.

On the side walls', which were divided by pillars, were a series of panels fifteen feet across which were decorated by an alternation of three motifs (No. 41): the pelican piercing her breast to feed her young with her own blood; the dove, a sign of hope, with the olive branch of peace in its beak; and, of special relevance to the Suffragette struggle, the broad arrow gilded and enclosed in a wreath of laurels of victory, symbolising Suffragette triumph through imprisonment.

The arches, which constituted, of course, part of the hall's fixtures, were

Nos. 35–37: Decorations for the Prince's Skating Rink Exhibition, May 1909.

37

No. 38: Decoration for the Prince's Skating Rink Exhibition, May, 1909.

likewise richly decorated with trees, green ivy, vines, and roses, clusters of ripe purple grapes, and brilliantly coloured orchid-winged butterflies.

The whole decoration was a labour of love, which engaged Sylvia from morning to night for, except when overlooking her assistants, she was constantly at work.[16]

Towards the end of the work she received a visit from Mr. Pethick Lawrence who inquired about the stalls for the exhibition. This came as a surprise to her as she had no idea that they were also her responsibility, but she at once rushed off with him to make the necessary arrangements.

Given the size of the murals, and the short time available, it is not surprising that the decorations were not completed until the very moment for them to be erected. Even then she accomplished the task only by labouring for two whole days and nights on end. (Her ability to work all night was one which she possessed throughout much of her life. I remember, as a child, often waking in the morning and going to her study to find her still at her desk, completing an article urgently needed by the printer.)

On the last day when Amy Browning entered the studio in the morning, Sylvia came down from the ladder tower and almost fainted on seeing that its

No. 39: Prince's Skating Rink Exhibition, May 1909. Detail of canvas at far end of the skating rink. PHOTO: INTERNATIONAL INSTITUTE OF SOCIAL HISTORY

Overleaf: No. 40: Prince's Skating Rink Exhibition, May 1909. Canvas at the far end of the skating rink. PHOTO: INTERNATIONAL INSTITUTE OF SOCIAL HISTORY

wheels had crushed two young mice that she and her assistants had tamed during their work.

The skating rink exhibition, which ran from May 13 to 26, 1909, was one in which the visitors were reminded of Votes for Women at every turn. Each person on entering the hall had pressed into his or her hand a ballot paper, and was invited to cast a vote on some question of the moment. At one end of the hall was a facsimile of a prison cell, in which sat a woman in second division prison dress who had actually been to Holloway, and could explain from personal knowledge the conditions to which the Suffragettes had been subjected, how they had to roll their bed, clean their tins, and so forth. Side by side with this was a replica of the much finer type of cell in which male political prisoners had been incarcerated. There were also glass cases with cartoon models of cabinet ministers in their various confrontations with the Suffragettes, and one of Mrs. Pankhurst leading a deputation to the House of Commons with frightened members of the government sheltering behind a group of stalwart police.[17]

119

No. 41: Prince's Skating Rink Exhibition, May 1909. The side wall canvases showing the pelican piercing her breast to feed her young; the broad arrow gilded and enclosed in a wreath of the laurels of victory; and the dove, a sign of hope.

Artistically the main interest of the exhibition was, however, the murals which were considered to symbolise the militant women's movement, and reproduced in Suffragette publications for several years to come. Though works of the moment rather than for posterity, Sylvia was thrilled to see her figures and decorations, which had been executed in such cramped conditions, extend over the vast walls of the skating rink. She felt that the work "bore the ordeal surprisingly well, and assumed an appearance of grace and brilliancy" which gave her great pleasure, despite her "acute consciousness of certain defects of detail". The creamy white walls, soaring figures, and the tracery of the arches, formed in her opinion a delightful background for the bright crowds of Suffragettes and their supporters that thronged the hall for a fortnight.[18]

In later years she often spoke to me, and others, of the excitement she had felt in producing those decorations. She recalled this half a century later when talking with the young Ethiopian artist, Afewerk Tekle, then engaged on his first great mural in St. George's Cathedral in Addis Ababa. She observed that he and other artists in newly developing countries were fortunate in the opportunity of accomplishing works of such grandeur, the more so in that theirs would be well-nigh permanent whereas hers at the skating rink were on view only for a few weeks. (Her original paintings were destroyed while her studio in Notting Hill Gate was being cleared up during one of her subsequent imprisonments as a Suffragette.)

Before the exhibition was over she left London, longing for leafy lanes and flowers, for a period of quiet study. She accordingly went, on Keir Hardie's suggestion, to Ightham in the Weald of Kent. Returning to London for the next bout of militancy, she later went to live for a short time in a cottage on Cinder Hill, near Penshurst, also in Kent, where she painted by day and wrote by night.

𝕵𝕰 9 Escalating Militancy; Oberammergau; the United States; Late Paintings

IN THE SUMMER OF 1909 the Suffragette movement, under Emmeline and Christabel's leadership, became increasingly militant. In June a woman sculptor, Marian Wallace Dunlop, entered the Parliament building where she endeavoured to print in St. Stephen's Hall an extract from the Bill of Rights stating that it was "the right of a subject to petition the King" and that all commitments and prosecutions for such petitioning were illegal. She was removed from the building, but, repeating the offence, was arrested, and sentenced to a month's imprisonment. Demanding the right to be considered a political prisoner she refused to eat until this was granted, and thus gained release after ninety-one hours, thereby acquiring a position in history as the first Suffragette hunger-striker. Towards the end of the month a group of women attempting to lobby the House of Commons deliberately broke the windows of a number of government offices, and inaugurated a phase of organised stone-throwing which was to become ever more common as the months passed.*

As the struggle became fiercer more and more women were imprisoned and subjected to increasingly severe sentences. But the women learned that they could further their cause, and effect their release, by hunger striking, and thus be able to resume the struggle. The Suffragettes, a group of dedicated women led by a determined yet autocratic leadership, were gripped in bitter and increasingly violent conflict with a most illiberal Liberal government.

Sylvia, the artist and Socialist, was by no means convinced that the road to women's emancipation lay through the type of organised violence favoured by her mother, elder sister and several other leading Suffragettes. "I believed, then

---

* Stones had actually been thrown at the Prime Minister's residence at 10 Downing Street by two women in the summer of the previous year, but Mrs. Pankhurst had stated that the action was unauthorised. One of these earlier stone throwers was Mary Leigh, who, forty years later, was photographed with my mother (see page 209) outside the House of Commons in a poster parade called to protest against proposals to return to Italy its former African colonies lost in World War II. *New Times and Ethiopia News.* (May 15, 1948).

as always," she afterwards wrote, "that the movement required, not more serious militancy by the few, but a stronger appeal to the great masses to join the struggle." Despite this conviction she felt unable to oppose the trend.

> I would rather have died at the stake than say one word against the actions of those who were in the throes of the fight. I knew but too surely that the militant women would be made to suffer renewed hardships for each act of more serious damage. Yet in the spate of that impetuous movement, they would rush enthusiastically to their martyrdom, and bless, as their truest saviours, the leaders who summoned them to each new ordeal. I realised how supremely difficult is the holding of calm thought and the sense of perspective at such a time, how readily one daring enthusiast influences another, and in the gathering momentum of numbers all are swept along. Posterity, I knew, would see the heroism of the militants and forget their damage, but in the present they would pay dearly.[1]

Though convinced that a wider popular approach than that adopted by some of the other Suffragettes would be more fruitful she continued to work in the WSPU, but snatched whatever free moments remained to return to her art. In what seemed might be a lull from militancy she went down in the summer of 1909 to the cottage on Cinder Hill, where after months of hard work in London she started to paint "for study and delight".[2]

It was possibly then that she produced two country scenes in oil. One (Plate XVI) depicts rolling hills descending towards the sea with a lane in the foreground. The other (not reproduced here), is of a sunlit road overhung by trees with two figures in the background. Also perhaps of this period is a pencil and watercolour study (No. 42) of a small girl standing in the kitchen seen through an open door.

Not long after her arrival at Cinder Hill the news broke that the government had responded to Suffragette hunger strikes by ordering that the women prisoners should be forcibly fed. This action, which was at first carried on in secret, was reported in the Press on September 18, 1909.

It was Keir Hardie, who, travelling down to Kent, informed her of the reaction of the House of Commons to the beginning of forcible feeding.* MP's, he explained, had merely laughed, though for his part the thought of it was making him ill. "I cannot stay here", Sylvia told him, "if it continues. I shall have to go to prison to stand by the others." "Of what use to make one more?" he asked, then added, "Finish what you are working on at least".[3]

---

* Writing of the forcible feeding introduced by the Liberal government to fight the Suffragettes, my mother later made the prophecy, up to now unfulfilled, that a representation of it would in time come to find a place on the walls of the House of Commons. E.S.Pankhurst, *The Suffragette Movement*, p. 389.

No. 42: Untitled. A small girl standing by a kitchen sink, seen through an open door.

However, her stay at Cinder Hill was in fact cut short by other news, for shortly afterwards on returning to the cottage from painting in a little wood, her canvas on her back, she found a telegram announcing that her brother Harry was seriously ill. He had been stricken with infantile paralysis and from the waist down was unable to move. She rushed to his bedside, his death bed as it turned out, and as her mother was away on a lecture tour in America she nursed him by herself for four months. Mrs. Pankhurst arrived home in time to see him breathe his last, early in January 1910. Sylvia chose that over his grave should be placed the words, "Blessed are the pure of heart."

No. 43: Self-Portrait.　PHOTO: NATIONAL PORTRAIT GALLERY

No. 44: Untitled.
Portrait of a young
woman.

While nursing Harry she continued to draw. The doctor who attended
Harry asked her to do a picture for him to give to his wife. It was to be called
"Affection". She did some sketches for him to choose how he would like the
subject represented. He did not, however, select any of them, but kept on
asking for more to choose from. "I came to the conclusion", she was later to
write to a friend, "he was not a very nice person and as I knew the time he was
likely to come ... I decided to be out when he called again. When one is quite
young and living alone one has to make such decisions at times." Most of the
studies were thrown away, but she kept one, of a woman sowing and a child,
for she was later to note, "I thought I might work it out some day."[4]

After her bereavement she returned to the cottage on Cinder Hill, cheer-
lessly collected her paintings and writings, took the furniture from her rooms in
Cheyne Walk, and moved to 3 Cambridge Lodge Studios, 42 Linden Gardens,
Notting Hill Gate.

No. 45: Untitled. Portrait
of a young working
woman.

It was probably at about this time that she drew a self-portrait (No. 43) in
red, white and black chalk, now in the National Portrait Gallery, and a series
of other young women's portraits in the same media and colours. Four of these
paintings are extant. One of them (No. 44), is unique in bearing a date –
1910, and, like two others (No. 45 and Plate XV) represents a young working
woman wearing a headscarf. Plate XV is unusual in that it portrays a woman
smiling with a tender and wistful expression. The fourth picture (Plate XV) is
of a woman's head and bare shoulders; the back of the frame bears the
uninformative words "A Study". These four works, which demonstrate the
artist's effort to obtain true likenesses of her models and are among the most
accomplished of her studies, bear her usual later signature "E. Sylvia
Pankhurst".

Another picture which dates from this period was her more detailed study
of Keir Hardie, a good portrait with kindly expressive eyes (No. 46). It was

The artist's signature as it appears on most of her later works.

done in charcoal, white chalk and red crayon, and was conceived as a "preliminary essay for a portrait in oil". As long as I can remember it hung in a prominent place in her study in Woodford Green. Before leaving for Ethiopia she presented it to the National Portrait Gallery, on which occasion she wrote that it was "regarded as a good likeness at the time (circa 1910)", though she regretted that "time and circumstances" had not permitted her to proceed to the oil portrait which she had hoped to develop from it. Later in a letter from Addis Ababa she was to write: "I am very conscious that this is only a sketch and was purely a preliminary study to assist me to do a painting which circumstances subsequently rendered impossible."*[5]

While in Linden Gardens she also began writing her first book, *The Suffragette: The History of the Women's Militant Suffrage Movement 1905–1910* which was to appear in May 1911 and bore on its cover her, by then, well-known portcullis emblem.

---

* In 1959 she told Elsa Fraenkel that the painting could not be executed, first because Keir Hardie was "too busy; then he became ill and died. I would never have ventured to offer it to the National Portrait Gallery," she added, "except for the fact that they had no portrait of him."

No. 46: Keir Hardie.

Meanwhile in the early summer of 1910, during a lull in Suffragette activity, she went, together with Annie Kenney, to Austria and southern Germany as a guest of Mrs. Pethick Lawrence. The three Suffragettes visited Innsbruck, and motored thence to Oberammergau for the famous passion play which is held every ten years. They were the guests of Anton Lang, the actor who played the part of Christ. At Parten Kirchen Sylvia visited a cottage workshop founded by a prisoner, a fact which took her thoughts back to the "drear wastefulness" of the English gaols, and made her impatient, as she said, to have the struggle for the vote over so that they could "move on to constructive work". She found the passion play with its thousand actors a "tremendous spectacle" and the choir "magnificent". It was, however, not the play itself which most pleased her, but, significantly enough, the life of the people, for Oberammergau was "a village of craftsmen; wood carvers, potters, fresco-painters, wherein was no poverty". There was moreover a famous carving school which interested her, and she was pleased to see the circulating library which brought books from Munich, and an art club which lent reproductions of artistic masterpieces to be hung in the home or for copying in fresco.[6] Such amenities had been sadly lacking in the industrial north of England.

Her visit to Oberammergau and Parten Kirchen is artistically well documented for the sketchbook she took with her, and two loose pages apparently from it, are preserved.

One of the loose leaves (No. 47) is a watercolour and gouache of a group of children, the boys in Tyrolean costume around a fountain in a village square. In the background are snow-clad mountains

Most of the sketchbook is devoted to watercolour and pencil studies of the various actors in the play. There is also a watercolour of the Crucifixion (No. 58). These studies cover a total of eighteen pages.

In the remaining studies, apparently made at Parten Kirchen, once again it is the working people and children who have caught her attention. The other loose sheet (Plate 11) is a gouache of a woman dressed in a bright blue smock painting figures on ornamental wooden plaques. The sketchbook also contains a watercolour sketch of a potter at work (No. 59) and another of a bare-footed youth pulling a hand cart (No. 60). There are in addition three watercolour sketches of poor children (Nos. 61–63).

Returning to Britain she immersed herself once more in the Suffragette movement, then in one of its most active periods. After the ninth "Women's Parliament", which met in November 1911, hundreds of women fought their

Opposite: No. 47: Untitled. A scene in the central square of an Alpine village.

48

49

50

51

52

53

54

55

56

57

Nos. 48–57: Studies for the Passion play in Oberammergau.

No. 59: Study of a potter at work.
Opposite: No. 58: Study of the Crucifixion.

No. 60: Study of a bare-footed youth.

way to the House of Commons, and there were no less than 285 arrests in three days. One of them was Sylvia's Aunt Mary who was by then frail and died two days after her release.[7]

Not long afterwards Sylvia sailed to the United States to speak on behalf of the suffrage movement in that country as well as her own. On the boat she worked to complete her book – and therefore left her paintbox behind. She was thrilled by the grandeur of the waves, as well as, on arrival at New York, by the jagged silhouette of the skyscrapers which seemed to her like a "ruined castle on the horizon". She was met by several leading American suffragists, among them Mrs. Stanton Blatch, and a flock of pressmen who kept her busy with interviews for three whole days. She received these journalists in relays, four to six at a time, and she found them exceedingly young, almost like schoolboys, she thought. Anxious that they should quote her correctly she asked them why they did not take notes, to which they indignantly replied: "We are not stenographers!" She rang for the "bell girl", ordered notebooks and pencils from the stationer's stall in the hotel, and then handed them out to

61

62

the young men who allowed her to suggest questions and then dictate answers. The resultant Press reports, she found, were excellent. Her lecture tour expanded, and she travelled all over the country as well as to New Brunswick in Canada.

While in the States she was invited to address the Senate and the House of Representatives in joint convention, the only other woman to have done so being Susan B. Anthony forty years earlier, and she also spoke to the Michigan legislature at Lansing and to the judiciary committees of Illinois and New York State.

Everywhere in America she was greeted with great enthusiasm, audiences streaming on to the platform in the American way to shake her hand and send greetings to the women's movement in Britain.

In the course of her tour she visited the Indian university in Arkansas, and incurred considerable wrath in the southern states by agreeing to speak at the Negro university in Tennessee. As one who had been imprisoned for the women's cause she was taken to visit many prisons, among them the terrible Harrison Street Jail in Chicago where she found the cells almost in darkness,

63

Nos. 61–63: Studies of poor children.

and the "Tank" in Tennessee where the inmates had no privacy and prowled backwards and forwards like wild beasts in the zoo. She noted that each prisoner had a WC without a lid which was flushed by a warden only once or twice a day.

Though shocked by much that she saw, particularly by the harsh extremes between rich and poor, as well as between white and black, she found the States exciting, and formed the impression that as a young country it was more receptive to new ideas than some of the older countries of Europe. For a moment she even thought that one day she might possibly become an American citizen.[8] I remember her speaking of all this forty years later, during the London blitz, when she recalled that had things been otherwise we might then have been American citizens. She was pleased, I think, that this had not been so, for had she gone to the States she would have missed her work in London's East End.

On her return to Britain she found the Suffragette movement "in a state of crisis", and she, now twenty-seven years old, felt there were areas of women's activity in which she "could and should do useful work". As she later recalled, she therefore decided "to give part as before and very soon my whole time to votes for women, thinking I could soon return to my work as an artist".[9]

It was at this time that she began work on a series of studies for what was, though she did not realise it at the time, to be her last, unfinished attempt at a big picture – a crowd of girls dancing with a background of trees. She made many elaborate studies for it, some of which still survive. They comprise half a dozen women in the nude in different poses, a study of the lower part of the female body with the legs and shoes, a study of feet, two studies of skirts and legs, a study of bare feet, five studies of legs and shoes, three studies of hands, in two cases holding objects, and four studies of clothed women, standing, walking or moving their hands. There were also two studies of children and two of trees and flowers.

She suspended this artistic activity, temporarily as she believed, to organise another WSPU exhibition which was held in the Portman Rooms just before Christmas 1911. The decorations used at the Prince's Skating Rink – described by *Votes for Women* as the "exquisite murals from the clever brush" of Sylvia

Opposite, Overleaf: Decorations originally made for the Prince's Skating Rink Exhibition of 1909 used once more at the Portman Rooms, Baker Street, in December 1911.
PHOTOS: MUSEUM OF LONDON

W.S.P.U, BAZAAR DEC., 1911. FK 4.

HERE IS A STALL
THAT YE ALL
MUST STOP AT.
BEFORE YE
GANG HAME
BUY A CUSHION
AND MAT !!!

AND
INVALIDS.

W.S.P.U. BAZAAR. 1911.

Pankhurst – had been stored for just such a contingency, and were again brought into use. As the ceiling sloped down at the sides sufficient depth could be obtained only by hanging the canvases several feet from the wall. This gave her the opportunity to make an aisle on each side with an open colonnade dividing it from the main hall. She produced the capitals in clay in her studio, and drew full size columns and bases which the bazaar fitters made at their workshop and cast, together with the capitals, in plaster. For the doors entering the main hall she designed and drew full size arches supported by smaller columns. On this occasion she was able to work without assistants or a special studio.[10] She later expressed herself fairly satisfied with the plasterwork which "looked as permanent as stone". The stallholders were dressed in eighteenth-century costume, and made to represent a variety of women types, gentlewomen, fisherwomen, market women, as well as weavers, workers of all kinds, a roast chestnut vendor, and a gipsy fortune-teller with two green birds, as well as a street crier, and a "zany" with his old fool's cap.

There was also a hand-worked roundabout and old-fashioned stall made by a carpenter from Sylvia's designs, based on an eighteenth-century hand-tinted book of costumes produced by the famous illustrator John Pine, which Keir Hardie had given her. The wearers of these costumes paid for them to be made up by voluntary workers at a studio in Kensington belonging to the Suffragette artists Georgina and Marie Brackenbury. There were also anti-suffrage coconut shies with representations of cabinet ministers, Lord Curzon, Mrs. Humphry Ward and other opponents of women's suffrage, and old London cries sung by Lady Sybil Smyth.[11]

The signs above the stalls, painted by Sylvia, were described in *Votes for Women* as particularly fine, and they turned the Portman Rooms "for the nonce in a village Market Hall".[12]

Suffragette militancy increased in the spring of 1912, when after a truce occasioned by hopes that the government would introduce a women's enfranchisement bill, Mrs. Pankhurst proclaimed on February 16 that "the argument of the broken window pane" was "the most valuable argument in modern politics".[13]

At her bidding dozens of women began smashing London shop windows with hammers, thereby creating thousands of pounds damage in a few minutes. Mrs. Pankhurst and the Pethick Lawrences were in consequence arrested, and Christabel fled to Paris in March to run the WSPU from France. Sylvia later visited her in Paris and found her entirely serene – but unwilling to listen to any ideas but her own. At her suggestion they therefore had little talk about

PLATE VIII An Old-fashioned Pottery Turning Jasper Ware.

PLATE IX Scotch Fisher Lassie Cutting Herrings.

PLATE X Untitled. Two women loading produce onto a horse-drawn cart.

PLATE XI Berwickshire Farmhands Threshing.

PLATE XII **In a Glasgow Cotton Mill: Minding a Pair of Fine Frames.**

64

65

66

67

Nos. 64–85: Studies for a large painting.

68

69

70

71

72

73

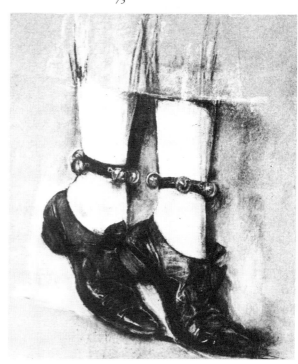

74

75

76

Suffragette tactics and went to look at pictures; Sylvia proposed a visit to the
Panthéon to see the paintings of Puvis de Chavannes.[14]

Mrs. Pankhurst and the Pethick Lawrences were charged at the Old
Bailey in May for their part in a conspiracy to effect wilful damage, and were
duly sentenced to nine months' imprisonment. Sylvia, who attended the
proceedings, found them "burlesque", and was saddened to think that so
much struggle was needed for so simple and obvious a reform as the defendants
demanded. Seeing how the courts of law were being used by the government in
its struggle to deny women their rights, she makes in passing one of her few
surviving comments on art when she refers critically to the "feeble, foolish

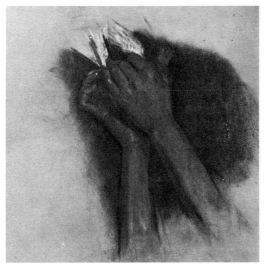

77

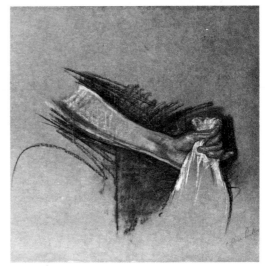

78

79

80

81

82

83

84

85

paintings" in the entrance to the Old Bailey. One of them, *The Golden Age,*
had been much talked of at the Royal College of Art because it had been
produced by one of the teachers, Professor Moira. To her it "seemed like a
silly gibe at the unhappy people dragged within those walls".[15]

That summer while her mother and the Pethick Lawrences were in prison
hunger striking – and later recovering in the countryside – and Christabel was
away in France, she prevailed on the local branches of WSPU to hold a series of
meetings in the principal parks and open spaces. These gatherings, which
attracted large crowds, culminated in a great Hyde Park demonstration on
July 14, 1912, which commemorated Mrs. Pankhurst's birthday as well as the
fall of the Bastille. Sylvia was actively engaged in preparing for this event,
working day and night on the decorations, which, significantly enough,
included scarlet caps of liberty and accurate replicas of the flags, banners and
even the mottoes used at the Peterloo meeting in Manchester in 1819. Such
decorations, which harked back to the earlier Radical movement, were displayed side by side with yellow-fringed banners in the Suffragette colours of
purple, white and green. The caps of liberty, my mother felt, were particularly
appropriate, for they had been prominent at Peterloo and other early nineteenth-century franchise meetings. Moreover "in the old days", she recalled,

the cap had been "shown on our coinage, being placed on the tip of Britannia's spear", though when the reformers used it as their emblem, "the reactionary government of the day pronounced it seditious and had it removed from the coinage." Many caps of liberty used by the reformers had indeed been made and presented by the women, "deputations of female Reformers usually making the presentation during great demonstrations".[16]

The display won general Suffragette approval, the journal *Votes for Women* commenting that both from the historian's and the artist's point of view Sylvia's decorations "called for the greatest admiration".[17] The artist herself was thrilled by the blaze of colour produced by the scarlet caps of liberty, gorgeously flaming on long poles, wide banners sailing over the crowd like sails on a sea of people, and all sorts of other colours: purple, white and green for the WSPU, orange and green for the Irish, black and white for the writers, green and gold with red dragons for the Welsh, black and brown for the tax resisters, red and white for Labour, and so on.[18]

Though much moved by the demonstration, Sylvia continued to deplore the fact that the movement seemed to be drifting towards increasing violence of the few rather than militancy by the many, and she realised that the struggle

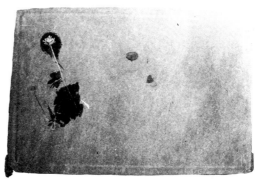

Left and Above: Nos. 88 and 89: Studies of flowers.

Opposite: Nos. 86 and 87: Studies of children.

would as a result be painful and long. Nevertheless she felt that "the psychology of politics necessitated that there should be no flinching" in the women's movement, and that, "above all, the tide of popular sympathy and support must not be allowed to recede." The movement, she thought, must not be allowed to "dwindle to a small group, however determined and heroic". To save the militants from years of imprisonment, or death by hunger strike and forcible feeding, a large popular agitation for the vote had to be "maintained at fever heat".[19]

Having by then saved sufficient money from her lecture tour in the United States she decided that she would give up all remunerative employment and devote all her time to the movement. The long contemplated decision to involve herself fully in the suffrage agitation having been taken she unreservedly entered the turmoil in which, as the Italian artist Emilia Folliero had warned her, there would be no place for art.

10 The East End; Hunger, Thirst and Sleep Strikes; Forcible Feeding; the "Cat and Mouse" Act

HAVING DECIDED TO DEVOTE HERSELF to full-time work in the women's movement, thus sadly at least temporarily abandoning her art, Sylvia felt at last free to act according to her own ideas, rather than to follow those sketched out by her sister in Paris.

The cleavage of opinion between the two sisters became apparent in the summer of 1912 when Christabel, in her wisdom, decided that the WSPU should embark on a policy of large-scale arson. One of the members of the government, C.E.Hobhouse, addressing a meeting in Bristol, had declared that the movement for women's suffrage had not been accompanied by any "great ebullition of popular feeling" as demonstrated by the burning of Nottingham Castle during the reform agitation of 1831–2. Christabel, incited and incensed by these words from a Liberal statesman, thought that her younger sister should have the honour of emulating the reformers of a century earlier, and accordingly sent a message to her from Paris asking quite bluntly if she would set fire to the castle. The idea of doing a stealthy deed of destruction, Sylvia afterwards explained, was "repugnant" to her, as she did not think such an act could assist the cause and she had "the unhappy sense of having been asked to do something morally wrong". She therefore replied that she would be willing only to "lead a torchlight procession to the castle, to fling my torch at it, and to call on others to do the same".[1] This proposal seemed, however, quite inadequate to Christabel who later published a dramatic picture of Nottingham Castle in flames with the caption in bold letters, "What men did to get the Vote."[2]

Sylvia, as an artist and humanitarian, as well as a believer in popularly based movements, rejected the "terrorist" tactics demanded by her sister. What was required, she believed, was "a broader and more confident appeal to the people" in order to make the movement a "genuine" one. "Secret incendiarism", the younger Pankhurst sister felt, merely "diluted enthusiasm, whittled away supporters, hardened opposition." She considered that it was, however, by then impossible to call a halt to militancy, and she "would not add one word to the chorus condemning those courageous girls who trusted implicitly in the wisdom of the Union".[3] Though she did not advocate militancy or take part in it, repudiation she would leave to others.

Division of opinion in the leadership of the WSPU erupted in October when the Pethick Lawrences refused to agree to the increased destruction ordained by Christabel and confirmed by Mrs. Pankhurst. The withdrawal of the Pethick-Lawrences from the organisation was, as Sylvia saw it, virtually inevitable in that as persons of wealth they could be called financially to account for damage carried out on behalf of the organisation whereas Mrs. Pankhurst in her relative poverty could only be subjected to imprisonment, while Christabel in Paris was immune from prosecution of any kind.

When the breach with the Pethick Lawrences occurred it was decided that the journal *Votes for Women* which they edited should no longer be the official organ of the WSPU, and that it be replaced as such by *The Suffragette* which Christabel was to run. Sylvia, whose thoughts ran back to the earlier abolition of the WSPU's constitution which had left decision making in unelected hands, was saddened by the dispute, even though she felt that the two sides differed less with each other than she as a democrat did with either of them. She declined to adopt a partisan attitude. When Mr. Pethick Lawrence wrote to ask her permission to continue using her design of the angel blowing a trumpet on the cover of *Votes for Women* she agreed.[4] For this act of family defiance she received the frowning reproach of her mother. Despite the artist's permission the design, presumably because it was the official insignia of the WSPU, was in fact no longer used by the paper.

Meanwhile, in accordance with her view that the movement required a broader and more popular base Sylvia had turned to the East End of London, which, as she saw it, constituted "the greatest homogeneous working-class area accessible to the House of Commons by popular demonstrations". Moreover, the emergence of a women's movement amid that "great abyss of poverty" would, she felt, be "a call and a rallying cry to the rise of similar movements in all parts of the country".

Believing that the suffrage movement had in the past always been largely middle-class, though the WSPU had begun otherwise, she felt that the taunt that the Suffragettes wanted a "Vote for Ladies" had produced a strong under-current in working class circles which had to be resisted. Quite apart from such

Sylvia speaking to an East End audience outside the newly opened suffragette headquarters in Bow, *c.* 1912. She had painted "Votes for Women" in Roman letters on the shop front.

tactical considerations, she hoped that the extension of the women's movement to the East End, and other such areas, would help "to fortify the position of the working woman" when the vote should actually be won, for "the existence of a strong, self-reliant movement amongst working women would be the greatest aid in safeguarding their rights in the day of settlement."

Emphasising this view, which was to have profound though entirely negative implications for her own artistic life, she was later to aver: "I was looking to the future; I wanted to rouse these women of the submerged mass to be, not merely the argument of more fortunate people, but to be fighters on their own account, despising mere platitudes and catch-cries, revolting against the hideous conditions about them, and demanding for themselves and their families a full share in the benefits of civilisation and progress."[5]

Imbued with such thoughts and aspirations she set out down the Bow Road, sometime in 1912, with Zelie Emerson, an American supporter, in search of rooms in which to establish offices for a popular movement. Finding an empty building to let, the two women polished and cleaned it until it shone. Then Sylvia, still the artist, mounted a ladder and wrote on the shop front the words "Votes for Women". She did so as beautifully as she knew how, in early Roman letters and gilt them with gold leaf. To see her, a woman, working on a ladder, she recalls, was "the astonishment, if not the scandal of the neighbour-hood".[6] The shop was, however, soon crowded with women telling of their everyday woes: rope makers, waste rubber cleaners, biscuit packers, women who plucked chickens often too "high" for canning, and those who made wooden seeds to be put in raspberry jam. Occupants of unhealthy tenements asked her to visit them and to expose their conditions.

Women flocked to her meetings and joined the organisation in large numbers. Anxious that her new friends, as she regarded them, should be active propagandists in their own struggle, not merely passive supporters as was so often the case with women's organisations in the past, she at once urged them to speak in meetings, took classes for them indoors, and induced them to address gatherings in the streets where people lived and in the markets. In this manner she laid the foundations for the popular type of women's organisation she had long favoured. It differed from the WSPU in being not an elitist group of militants, but a much broader movement, embracing a large section of the population in the area. She watched this movement grow, she was later to assert, "with the anxious intensity of a nurse by the bedside of a loved patient fighting for life". She, was, however, conscious that for her personally involve-ment in the East End was "no light-hearted adventure", for through it she was steadily moving further from her "chosen mission", from the "artist's work which gave me a satisfaction and pleasure found in nothing else".[7]

Undeterred by such thoughts she continued her work with the East End women in the spirit of her father's old adage "Life is nothing without enthusiasms." On January 14, 1913, she took a deputation of by then highly articulate working women to the WSPU headquarters whence they made their way to Whitehall to plead their case before two members of the cabinet, Sir Edward Grey and Lloyd George.

A few hours later, learning that the Speaker of the House of Commons was refusing to allow a women's suffrage amendment bill to be introduced despite earlier government promises to the contrary, she was filled with indignation. Feeling the need to protest she rushed to her rooms in Linden

Gardens where she groped in the dark courtyard in search of a stone, but, finding only lumps of concrete, seized some of them, and made her way to Parliament without any idea as to where to throw them. On reaching St. Stephen's Hall she considered, as an artist no less than as a Suffragette, where to take aim. It was unthinkable, she felt, to attack a stained glass window, a statue, or other work of an artist's loving toil. At that point, however, she caught sight of a huge picture which seemed to her "feebly unattractive", its subject making "no impression" on her. Anyway, it was covered by a great expanse of glass so the picture itself would not suffer. Accordingly she hurled one of the big lumps in her pocket. It glanced off the glass, leaving not a scratch, but shattered itself on the paving, thus creating a deafening noise in the stone building. Policemen rushed upon her and took her into custody but the Speaker decided to take no action against her and she was promptly released. She was told of this decision by Keir Hardie who rushed to bring her the news. He was glad, he said, that she had reacted to the Speaker's action so promptly, and wished that every woman in the country had done the same. He then conducted her from the Parliament precincts as though she was an honoured guest. The picture against which she had thrown the stone was, curiously enough, one of Speaker Finch attempting to adjourn the House in 1629 in obedience to the wish of the king, and being held in his chair by MPs to compel him to put the resolution against tonnage and poundage.[8] Her act of violence, though symbolic, was by Suffragette standards of the day very modest, for at about this time supporters of the WSPU's militant line hacked up thirteen pictures in the Manchester Art Gallery and burnt several stately homes to the ground.*

The East End movement was meanwhile growing apace. Early in February a new headquarters for it was established at 321 Bow Road. A week later, on February 14, Sylvia and Zelie Emerson led a procession through the district, and ceremonially threw some stones. They were both arrested, and sentenced to six weeks imprisonment. They began a hunger and thirst strike, but were speedily released as Mrs. Pankhurst paid the fine.

---

* Suffragettes were later, in 1914, to do even greater damage to works of art. *The Rokeby Venus*, attributed to Velasquez – falsely in Sylvia's opinion – and purchased by the National Gallery for £45,000, Romney's *Master Thornhill* in the Birmingham Art Gallery, and Carlyle's portrait by Millais in the National Portrait Gallery were all damaged. A Bartolozzi drawing in the Doré Gallery was completely ruined, while the stained glass window in St. George's, Hanover Square, was damaged. E.S.Pankhurst, *The Suffragette Movement*, p. 544.

A few days later they held another meeting, at the obelisk by Bow Church, followed by further stone throwing to obtain arrest. Sylvia and five other protestors were subsequently seized by the police. Again they went on hunger and thirst strike. For the first two days the prison authorities tried to tempt her by placing food in the cell such as was never normally seen at Holloway Prison. The varied colours diverted her artist's eye, but, she had no more inclination to eat, she said, than if they had been a still life picture. On the third day two prison doctors sounded her heart, felt her pulse, and then told her that they had no alternative but to feed her by force. Six wardresses flung her on her back on the bed, and held her down firmly by shoulders and wrists, hips, knees and ankles. Her mouth was forced open, and she felt a steel instrument pushed into it. The screw was then turned to prise open her jaws. A feeding tube was then thrust down her throat. She vomited as the contraption was removed. She was left on her bed, gasping for breath and sobbing convulsively.

This routine of tube-feeding continued day after day. Her back and head ached almost continuously – but she soon discovered that by thrusting her hand down her mouth she could make herself vomit, thus largely negating the warders' efforts to feed her. As soon as she could pull herself together after the forcible feeding she would therefore struggle to bring up what they had forced into her. After some days the flesh around her eyes became increasingly painful, and she shrank from the light. She noticed that the officials who passed by her door began to stop and stare at her.

Subjected to such torture, and denied access to writing paper, let alone drawing materials, there was no opportunity of practising her art as on former imprisonments. She now had resort only to a slate. Once, to divert herself, she drew an illustration to Omar Khayyám's "Awake for morning in the bowl of night has flung the stone that puts the stars to flight," a passage which was also a favourite of Christabel's. On another occasion, influenced by the Bible to which she had access as prisoner, she was inspired by Ezekiel XXXIV, and sought to illustrate the passage about the shepherds who have eaten the fat and clothed themselves in the wool, but have neither cared for the sick nor sought the lost animals, so that the flock, for lack of a shepherd, has been scattered and become meat to all the beasts of the field. She conjured up the impression of a group of shepherds feasting together on the edge of a cliff by a fire at which they roasted a young lamb. The animal had caught its horns in the branches of a tree overhanging the precipice, while many of the flock had fallen, and were lying dead on the rocks below. She saw the theme in contemporary terms, for though the shepherds were dressed like those of old, their faces were

164

those of cabinet ministers. Such pictures were, however, far from satisfying, for, she was afterwards to declare, "a slate is a dismal thing to draw on; one cannot retain one's zest in making drawings to rub out." She therefore turned to writing, and, fearing too quickly to exhaust the few carefully guarded pieces of toilet paper at her disposal, wrote in verse as the most concentrated form of expression. She began a play on the biblical story of David and Bethsheba, the pages of which were, however, subsequently lost.[9]

During this time she slept but little, and lay thinking: passages she had read from the Bible during the day came back to her as resplendent visions, such as that evoked by the words, "How beautiful upon the mountains are the feet of him that bringeth good tidings, that publisheth of peace."

Being prevented by forcible feeding from gaining speedy release by the then time-honoured practice of hunger striking, she determined on the novel expedient of a sleep and rest strike. She accordingly began walking up and down the cell until she fell; but since she did not faint, she got up and continued walking. She did this for a total of twenty-eight hours – until the Home Office doctors ordered her to be freed.

While Sylvia was still in gaol her mother was charged with inciting her followers to destroy property. Mrs. Pankhurst was duly sentenced to three years' penal servitude, whereupon she too immediately began a hunger strike – and was freed after nine days.

The government at about this time introduced the Prisoners' Temporary Discharge for Ill Health Act, always referred to by the Suffragettes as the "Cat and Mouse" Act, which gave the Home Secretary the power to release hunger strikers to allow them to recover, usually for a period of five to seven days, and then to take them once more to prison, freeing and re-arresting them until their entire sentence had been served. Sylvia worked behind the scenes to set up a "Cat and Mouse" appeal committee under Sir Edward Burke and two eminent surgeons, Sir Victor Horsley and Mr. Mansell-Moulin. Her closest friend and co-worker in this period was Norah Smyth, a niece of the musician Dr. Ethel Smyth, and a woman with whom she was soon to share a lodging in the East End.

Meanwhile, on June 4, 1913, Derby Day, there occurred a tragedy which will ever be remembered in connection with the Suffragette movement. On that day one of the militants, Emily Wilding Davison, rushed onto the race course at Epsom in an attempt to stop the King's horse. She was in an instant incurably injured and died four days later without regaining consciousness.

Though the police sought to prevent a demonstration at her funeral, a long procession of women marched to St. George's Church, Hart Street, and the nearby streets were lined with silent respectful crowds.

Mrs. Pankhurst planned to attend the ceremony and my mother was to go with her, but the former's prison licence having expired, she was snatched away by the police earlier that day. Sylvia, who walked with hunger strikers to the church, in the stress of the moment, penned the following somewhat incoherent lines which she sent to the *Daily Mail*:

> O Deed Majestic! O triumphant death!
>
> The crowded, trivial race-course and the glaring sun.
>
> The swift rush out into the horror of horses' hoofs; a frantic, clinging impact.
>
> Then, unseen, the column of flame that rises up to Heaven as the great heart bursts – the ascending spirit is set free.
>
> O deed of infinite majesty! Great heart that none could ever know!
>
> Parliament sits – a House of Mockery! It proses on without a word of that great act, or the great Cause for which she gave her life.
>
> The world goes on as though it could not heed.
>
> They carry the poor broken body through the streets, women in white with lilies, clergy in their robes, poor people who have gone without some needed thing even to come thus far to follow her.
>
> All those four miles the roads are thronged with crowds who wait, silent and with bared heads to see her pass.
>
> One should be there – another woman whom they dragged back from following her, back to the gaol where with starvation and weakness she fights strong powers that be.
>
> O dullard minds in power that cannot see great Freedom's history making; great tragic acts under their very eyes!
>
> Parliament sat to govern us the while, and not a man rose to speak of it.[10]

These words were written in the stress of the moment. Asked afterwards to authenticate them prior to their appearance in the newspaper, she chose not to do so. They therefore remained unpublished.

Shortly afterwards, on June 29, she addressed a meeting in Trafalgar Square where she called on the crowd to march in procession to Downing Street to hoot the Prime Minister, Herbert Asquith, and his Cabinet for having chosen to resort to such extremes against women rather than granting them citizenship. The East Enders responded with enthusiasm, there were numerous scuffles with the police, followed by several arrests.

A few days later, while working in her studio in Linden Gardens, she received a summons under a statute of Edward III to appear in court, as "a disturber of the peace of our Lord and the King". Ignoring the summons, and thus courting arrest, she later went to a meeting in Bow at which she had already been billed to speak. The audience, knowing that an order had been issued for her arrest, on seeing her rose to its feet, cheering and waving their hands, while friends slammed and barricaded the doors. A strong force of police had in the meantime gathered outside. When the speeches were over the people formed a bodyguard to protect her, and together they pushed their way out. Dozens of men and women held their arms around her and each other. Detectives nevertheless fought their way through the crush, and at length succeeded in arresting her. She was sentenced to three months' imprisonment.

Entering gaol on the Tuesday she at once adopted a hunger and thirst strike, but finding that this did not produce sufficiently fast a deterioration in her health to ensure her release in time for a meeting she was to address in Bromley Public Hall on the following Monday, she decided again to have resort to a sleep and rest strike. She began walking about her cell on Friday, and, being already much debilitated by her earlier imprisonment and forcible feeding, she began to faint on Saturday. She was released on Sunday.

On leaving prison she was driven by taxi, in the company of two ward-resses, to the home of two of her supporters – Mr. and Mrs. Payne, home-workers in the shoe-making trade, who lived at 28 Ford Road, Bow. It was, as she afterwards recalled, "a typical little East End house in a typical little street, the front door opening directly from the pavement, with not an inch of ground to withdraw its windows from the passer-by". There she was welcomed, she says, "by the kindest of kind people" who had put their double bed for her in the front parlour, and although scarcely able to afford the sacrifice, for three days refrained from work lest she was disturbed by the sound of their tools.[11]

On the evening after her release she attended her meeting, and found the hall packed, and thousands of people crowded outside. They cheered her, crying, "We'll never let them take you back!" "Votes for women this year!" and "Down with the 'Cat and Mouse' Act!"

On July 21, though her "Cat and Mouse" release had expired, she was again due to speak at Bromley Public Hall. She was smuggled into the building through police waiting to arrest her, and rushed onto the platform. There, with an element of drama, she declared: "They say that life is sweet and liberty is precious; there is no liberty for us so long as the majority of our people lead wretched lives. Unless we can free them from the chains of poverty, life to us is not worth preserving, and I, for one, would rather leave this world." Then she jumped from the platform into the body of the hall, and escaped with the crowd.

A few days later she spoke at Canning Town Public Hall, where she went in disguise. The people once more cheered her, and hissed the detectives who were thrust from the building. She again managed to escape the detectives in the darkness of the night.

On July 27, she decided to speak as announced in Trafalgar Square in broad daylight. She arrived in the square again in disguise dressed in an American shepherd's plaid coat and shirt stuffed with newspapers across the chest. When the time came for her to address the crowd she tore off her disguise, amid a great waving of hands and a roar of cheering.

After her speech the assembly adopted by acclaim a resolution to carry a "Women's Declaration of Independence" to Downing Street. Then she jumped from the plinth and was caught by the people below. Before the police could bring up their massed forces which were waiting in the side streets, the crowd swept from the square into Parliament Street. Detectives were everywhere in the crowd, but the people always knew them and hustled them away. There was, she recalls, "a strange deep growling sound in the crowd about me I had never heard before: the sound of angry men. At the top of Whitehall, mounted police met us; we rushed between. The people protecting me gathered in a thick bunch with their arms about each other, thrusting the horses aside." Police reinforcements, however, then dashed forward, beating their way through the people, and at last seized her.

The demonstration was nevertheless accounted a great success. The journalist H. W. Nevinson called her action at this time in throwing herself on the "genuine chivalry and good sense" of the workers in the East End "a stroke of genius", and went on: "We have all the working classes now, not only favourable, but zealous. After the battle of Valmy, when the national troops of the French Revolution held in check the hirelings of official Europe, Goethe said to his friends: 'To-day marks a turning-point in history, and we can say we were present at it.' We who were in the Square last Sunday can say the same."

Sylvia, back meanwhile in Holloway Prison, in the same cell as before, once again adopted the hunger, thirst and sleep strike from Sunday till Friday when she developed a fever and was released.

Eluding the police she was able to attend another great Trafalgar Square meeting on August 10, and was again arrested while leading crowds in

168

Downing Street. Again she struck in prison, and was released after four days. These events created considerable excitement in the East End, where continuous meetings began to be held.

The women of the East End were in fact rallying to her wing of the Suffragette movement in ever increasing numbers. Early in June the branches she had formed in the area were, despite the disapproval of Christabel in Paris, brought together to constitute the East London Federation of the WSPU.

Such activity left her no time to draw or paint, but she still craved for her art. By then debilitated by her repeated hunger, thirst and sleep strikes she was much incapacitated by pain, and accordingly agreed in the summer of 1913 to leave London for a time. Though subject to arrest, she slipped away with Norah Smyth to Copenhagen to lecture to the Danish Women's Federation, and gave interviews to the Danish and Norwegian Press. They stayed in a Norwegian farmhouse and she went about sketching the people, the majestic scenery, and the old wooden buildings with their intricate carvings.[12]

None of her studies of this period seem, however, to have survived.

She was soon back in England, and on October 13 went, once more in disguise, to an East End meeting called to welcome her back. In the middle of her speech she heard the crowd in extraordinary agitation cry out to her, "Jump, Sylvia, jump!" She leaped from the platform as detectives armed with sticks poured onto the platform from the rear. Members of the audience fought back with benches and chairs as she made her way out of the building. People kept changing hats with her to make it more difficult for her to be identified from afar.

Outside the hall mounted police with rearing horses drove the crowd before them. The mass scattered, reformed and were scattered again. She was conducted through this scene of disorder, as she later often related with some amusement, by "Kosher" Hunt, a noted East End prize-fighter, who had dashed to her rescue. "In this commotion", she wrote, "a uniformed constable recognised me. I saw him start, and raise his arm to stop me passing, then he drew back – from fear or pity? I thought the latter." In the dark she made her escape.[13]

The following evening she went, disguised as a poor woman carrying a "baby" in her arms, to speak at Poplar Town Hall. She was, however, spotted by the police, and speedily arrested, despite efforts by the crowd to secure her release. Another hunger and thirst strike followed, cut short by a sleep strike timed to obtain her release in time for her next appointment nine days later.

Then followed in some ways the most remarkable action of all, and one designed to forge a link between the women's and workers' movements. She agreed, though without consulting her mother or sister, to speak at a large Albert Hall meeting called to demand the release from prison of James Larkin, a Liverpool Irishman who had organised a number of successful strikes in Dublin, then seething with Home Rule agitation. She received immense applause, and succeeded with little difficulty in escaping amid the crowd of ten thousand people. The Labour *Daily Herald* underlined the significance of her presence on the platform observing: "Every day the industrial rebels and the suffrage rebels march nearer together."[14]

At her next meeting, at Bow Baths, she again managed to get to the hall, address the audience, and escape, despite the presence of a force of three hundred mounted police sent to arrest her. Further meetings were held at the Bow Palace Music Hall and Shoreditch Town Hall, but at the latter gathering she was again arrested only to be released after a six-day strike at the conclusion of which she addressed a meeting at Covent Garden. She was then once more seized by the police, on January 4, 1914, but was freed as usual two days later.

In this way she endured ten successive hunger and thirst strikes between June 1913 and June 1914. Such activity in and out of prison* left her almost completely exhausted, and with no time for painting.

---

* During her numerous incarcerations she learned much about the life of the prison populace which was vividly revealed in the tragic messages scratched on cell walls: "I only did it for my poor children", or "Oh, God, when shall I know my fate?" E.S.Pankhurst, *The Suffragette Movement*, p. 441.

11 The East London Federation of Suffragettes; the *Woman's Dreadnought*; Forcing the Prime Minister to Receive a Deputation; the End of an Artistic Career

A T THE BEGINNING OF JANUARY 1914, though then in hiding and subject to re-arrest under the "Cat and Mouse" Act, Sylvia travelled to Paris with Norah Smyth at the request of Mrs. Pankhurst and Christabel. It was there intimated to her that the East London Federation was too working class in composition and democratic in organisation to remain within the framework of the WSPU. Christabel chided her younger sister saying, "You have a democratic constitution for your federation; we do not agree with that." Moreover, she urged that a movement of working women was of little use, for the latter were too weak. "We want picked women," she said, "the very strongest and the most intelligent." Speaking directly to Sylvia, she added, "You have your own ideas. We do not want that; we want all our women to take their instructions and walk in step like an army!" Mrs. Pankhurst and Christabel thereupon ordered the East London movement to sever itself from the WSPU, whereupon the East Enders changed their name to the East London Federation of Suffragettes. They chose for their colours the old purple, white and green, to which they added red, a colour already used on the red Suffragette caps of liberty. Mrs Pankhurst protested that the name Suffragettes should be reserved for her organisation, but Sylvia insisted that her members had themselves decided on the name and she would not interfere to alter it.[1] The breach led to an extension of Suffragette activity, for, whereas Christabel sought to rely on women, and spurned the help of men, Sylvia appealed to the workers of both sexes.[2]

No sooner had the federation gained its autonomy than Zelie Emerson urged Sylvia to found a newspaper. A meeting was called, and the members chose the name *Woman's Dreadnought* – this being a time when Dreadnought battleships were much in the news.

The first issue appeared on March 21, 1914. Sylvia's editorial policy was to provide a medium through which working women, however unlettered, might express themselves, and find their interests defended. The paper was as far as possible written from life, without dry arguments, and was so popular that it soon achieved a weekly circulation of twenty thousand copies. Editing the paper, writing for it, proof-reading, and raising funds for it, soon became one of Sylvia's main preoccupations. On occasion she wrote for it secretly in prison, and when the date of publication approached fought by the sleep strike to get free in time to bring it out.

She had by this time moved to 400 Old Ford Road which served as head-quarters for the East London Federation, as well as her own home, and that of her then principal co-worker Norah Smyth and Mr. and Mrs. Payne. The building had formerly been a school and later a factory and it had a hall capable of holding about three hundred people.

Meanwhile meetings followed meetings. At one of them, on March 8, she was seized by some policemen on foot assisted by mounted police. The officers tried to take her away by bus, but the conductor refused to allow them on board. "No, no! you shan't take her on here! I won't help you take her!" he cried. She was, however, dashed back to Holloway Prison by taxi while the crowd fought its way on to Downing Street.

On her release she planned a march on Westminster Abbey, to be followed by public prayer on "Mothering Sunday". By this time she was so weakened by constant hunger, thirst and sleep strikes that she was obliged to travel in a spinal chair borrowed from the Cripples' Institute. On the day in question she was, however, carried shoulder high by the crowd past policemen too few in numbers to seize her in so vast a throng. On reaching the abbey they found the door closed, but a friendly clergyman, Parson Wills, the leader of the procession, held a service outside.

She then smuggled herself out of the country to lecture in the Austrian empire – but was banned from entering the Kaiser's Germany. In Budapest she was much impressed by the newly built workers' suburb which far surpassed in comfort and architectural beauty any dwellings of the kind she had ever seen. She went on to Vienna where after addressing a women's meeting she did some sightseeing: she was thrilled with the city's old Gothic cathedral with its richly sculptured walls and jewel-like windows, and by the picture galleries which she considered "splendid".[3]

Weakened by her hunger strikes, Sylvia, in a long chair, is carried out of a meeting by her supporters to see the Prime Minister, Herbert Asquith, June 10, 1914.

Returning to England, where she moved into her new home in the Old Ford Road, she addressed further meetings in Bow, but was seized while organising a "Women's May Day" procession in which she was to march in the centre of twenty women chained to each other. They refused to hand over the keys, and the padlocks had to be smashed on their hands by police batons, while the crowd struggled to secure the release of their leaders. "We received many a blow during the process," she records, "and any woman who attempted to hinder the work had her face pinched, her hair pulled, arms twisted and thumbs bent back." The populace meanwhile repeatedly charged the mounted police who fought back with truncheons. Part of the park railings were destroyed. As they took her to prison by taxi one of the policemen said to her, significantly, "the people fight for you and are willing to make sacrifices for the cause."

Another strike brought speedy release on May 30, whereupon she determined to make a final appeal to Prime Minister Asquith. Until then he had argued that the demand for the vote had come only from a handful of women, not from the masses. She therefore decided to confront him with a deputation of women popularly elected from one of her great East End rallies. She planned to accompany the delegation which, she believed, would almost certainly be refused access to the Prime Minister. Since her "Cat and Mouse" licence had expired she would be arrested, but she determined that she would continue a hunger and thirst strike, inside or outside prison until the deputation was received. "Asquith," she thought, "might maintain his refusal to the bitter end; he had always been stubborn. In that case I must leave others to carry on the fight. I did not want to die and leave all we hope to do – yet I was willing to die if it might help to ensure the victory."

She accordingly wrote to the Prime Minister asking him to receive a deputation. When this was, as she anticipated, refused, she replied that he had "on many occasions stated that he was unaware of any popular demand for Votes for Women", and continued:

> Do you realise that since I was arrested for a speech to the people who had come in procession from East London to Trafalgar Square, in which I asked them to go to your house in Downing Street to hoot you for your refusal to give votes to women, I have spoken at dozens of immense public meetings when liable to re-arrest by the police; and in each case the general public, who have come quite freely and without tickets or payment, into the largest halls of those districts, have rallied round me, to a man and to a woman, to protect me from the police, although they have incurred many hard blows and risked imprisonment in doing so ?

Explaining that "a large proportion of the women of East London" were "living under terrible conditions", and were "impatient to take part in moulding the conditions under which they have to live", she declared:

> I regard this deputation as of such importance that I have determined, should you refuse to receive the deputation and I be snatched away from the people, as I probably shall be, and taken back to Holloway, my 'Cat and Mouse' licence having expired, I will not merely hunger strike in Holloway, as I have done eight times under this present sentence, but when I am released, I shall continue my strike at the door of the Strangers' Entrance to the House of Commons, and shall not take either food or water until you agree to receive this deputation. I know very well from what has happened in the past that I am risking my life in coming to this conclusion, because, so far, you have almost invariably refused the appeals which suffragists have made to you. At the same time I feel it is my duty to take this course, and I shall not give way, although it may end in my death.[4]

On receipt of this letter Asquith, as she expected, again refused to receive the deputation. When she announced this at the next of her meetings, on June 10 the women broke out weeping. The Reverend Wills asked to be allowed to pray. Sylvia declared her intention to proceed to the House of Commons, and was taken out of the meeting on a long chair carried in procession by a group of supporters, among them the journalist Nevinson. At a narrow point in the road the police broke through the crowd, and she was arrested.

The next day the hunger strike was discussed in the House of Commons. The Home Secretary declared that he had been advised to let Suffragette hunger strikers die, but he felt that "for every woman who died there would be scores who would come forward for the honour, as they would deem it, of the crown of martyrdom," and "when there were twenty, thirty, forty or more deaths in prison, you would have a violent reaction of public opinion." The whole question, he declared, was "a phenomenon without precedent in our history".

Meanwhile in prison, Sylvia, who had been arrested on June 10, remained on hunger and thirst strike until June 18 when the wardresses took her to her home in the Old Ford Road. A crowd had already collected, the womenfolk once more weeping. She at once asked Norah Smyth to drive her to the House of Commons where a small group of supporters had assembled by the statue of Richard the Lionheart. Keir Hardie and another MP suggested that it would be more convenient for her to wait in St. Stephen's Hall, but this was not possible as she had been banned from entering the Parliament on account of her earlier demonstration. She therefore crawled, with the help of the crowd, towards the Strangers' Entrance, but, being stopped by the police, situated herself near Cromwell's statue. Nevinson later wrote:

> I stood beside her, very helpless, while she lay on the steps, apparently dying, and the police, perhaps in pity, hesitated to drive her away. At last, to my infinite relief, Keir Hardie came out of the House, and on hearing from me what the situation was, stood with me. George Lansbury joined us and hastened to see Mr. Asquith, who consented to receive six working women in two days time.

After much persuasion, Sylvia agreed to accept the promise, and, with Keir Hardie's help, Nevinson lifted her into a taxi.[5]

As soon as it was known that Asquith had agreed to receive the deputation the crowd was gripped with great excitement. Everyone around her was laughing with joy, and then there were shouts of "We are winning! We are winning!" Driving back to her home in the Old Ford Road, she asked if they could stop on the way to have her first drink of water after eight days.

This strike, and the Prime Minister's agreement to meet with the deputation, represented an important turning point in the struggle. Nevinson remarked that the arrival of the working women in Downing Street had "a

GUARANTEED WEEKLY CIRCULATION—20,000 COPIES.

THE WOMAN'S DREADNOUGHT

Published by the East London Federation of the Suffragettes.
Edited by SYLVIA PANKHURST.

No. 14.   SATURDAY, JUNE 20TH, 1914.   PRICE ONE HALFPENNY.

NO PRICE TOO GREAT TO PAY FOR FREEDOM.

THIS WEEK'S MEETINGS.

Sunday, June 21st, 3 p.m.—Victoria Park.
7.30 p.m.—The Women's Hall, 400 Old Ford Rd., Bow—Dr. Mansell-Moullin, Mrs. Merivale Meyer.
Monday, June 22nd, 3 p.m.—The Women's Hall, 400 Old Ford Rd., Bow—Members' meeting.
8 p.m.—The Women's Hall, 400 Old Ford Rd., Bow—Speakers' Class.
8.30 p.m.—Swiss Cottage, S. Hackney—Miss Holmes.
8 p.m.—Priscilla Rd., Bow.
8 p.m.—Freemason's Rd., Canning Town—Mrs. Laski.
Tuesday, June 23rd, 8 p.m.—Dock Gates, Poplar—Mr. Mewitt.
8 p.m.—Limehouse, Burdett Rd., and Coutts Rd.
Wednesday, June 24th, 8 p.m.—319 East India Dock Rd., Poplar—Miss Jacobs.
8 p.m.—Crowder's Hall, 178 Bow Rd.—Mrs. Tyson.
8 p.m.—Chrisp St. & Charles St., Bromley.
Thursday, June 25th, 3 p.m.—319 East India Dock Rd., Poplar—Miss Canning.
3 p.m.—Deacon's Vestry, Burdett Rd., Limehouse.
8 p.m.—124 Barking Rd., Canning Town.
8 p.m.—Woodstock Rd., Poplar.
Friday, June 26th, 8 p.m.—Ford Rd., Bow.
8 p.m.—Piggott St., Poplar—Mr. Jane.
8 p.m.—Beckton Rd., Canning Town—Mrs. Laski.
8 p.m.—The Women's Hall, 400 Old Ford Rd., Bow—Members' Meeting.
Sunday, June 28th, 5 p.m.—Trafalgar Square F.C.S.U. Demonstration.

HOW ASQUITH SHIRKS.

We print below the correspondence which passed between the members of the East London deputation and the Prime Minister who is partly supported by women's money and one of whose duties it is to listen to the grievances of His Majesty's subjects and devise a means of redressing them. The wording of Mr. Asquith's second letter is especially significant as showing that he has not grasped the fundamental duties of his position. He says that *the views of the Government* were explained at considerable length. It seems that Mr. Asquith has yet to learn that deputations do not visit him to hear his views on any subject but to lay the views of the people he is supposed to represent before him.

[COPY.]

June 12th, 1914.

Dear Sir,—As members of the deputation who came to the House to see you on Wednesday last, we must express very strongly our dissatisfaction at not being received by you. We can see no reason why you should not see us and hear what we (as working women) have to say about the franchise. You cannot possibly know what the views of the people are if you will not listen to them. You have never received a deputation of working women on this question; therefore, until you know the why and

he is unable to receive a deputation, and he regrets that he is unable to reconsider this decision. As you are, doubtless, aware, deputations have been received by the Prime Minister and other Members of the Cabinet, which were representative of the constitutional organisations connected with the Women's Suffrage Movement. At nearly all these deputations working women were either present or their opinion represented. The views of the Government were explained to the members of the deputations at considerable length, and no change has taken place in the situation since then.

The Prime Minister has been compelled to refuse requests from a large number of bodies for similar deputations, and, after careful consideration of all the circumstances,

convince the Premier where he is wrong. Just a word from him, consenting to receive our deputation, would save that noble little woman, Sylvia Pankhurst, from death by starvation. Should she die, it will be a very serious matter, for ours is a true Socialist's spirit. 'An injury to one is an injury to all.' I trust you will act as soon as possible, as delay is dangerous."

The letter, to which the name and address of the writer were appended, has received an unsatisfactory and evasive reply. Others who have written to Mr. Thorne have received exactly the same answer, showing that he does not even consider his constituents' letters individually, but has supplied his secretary with a draft copy to be used to all who write on this subject.

IS SHE TO DIE ?

He was followed by Mrs. Parsons, who put the whole matter from the standpoint of the East London working woman.

Then came an appeal for money from the chair. The response was prompt and generous, several cheques being handed up in addition to the ordinary collection.

Miss Evelyn Sharp was the next speaker, she also spoke as a witness of the events on the night of Miss Pankhurst's arrest, and dwelt on the significance of the large numbers of working men whose presence on that occasion proved that they are making this question their own.

As she concluded with a tribute to George Lansbury and his gallant challenge to his namesake George V. the challenger himself appeared on the platform, and was greeted with vigorous applause. His appeal was especially to the men, and he urged upon them to call at the House of Commons to see their respective members of Parliament, and ask them to put pressure upon Mr. Asquith. He satirised the Press for their habitual misrepresentation of everything in connection with the movement for Freedom.

Miss Amy Hicks made a brief appeal for workers, and emphasised the need for immediate action at this crisis.

The resolution was carried unanimously and before the meeting broke up the enthusiasm that had been aroused found an outlet in many promises of very practical help.

McKENNA'S TRIBUTE TO THE MILITANTS.

On Thursday, June 11th, the debate on the Home Office took place. This was chiefly concerned with the Suffragettes and the methods to be employed to stop their activities.

Mr. McKenna said that: "The present situation was a phenomenon absolutely without precedent, and then discussed four alternatives for dealing with it.

1. Let them die (which was the most popular).
2. Deport them.
3. Treat them as lunatics.
4. Give them the franchise.

LET THEM DIE.

"Those who say 'Let them die if they choose to starve themselves,' usually base their views on the conviction that if they themselves were told that they would left to die they

The front page of the *Woman's Dreadnought* of June 20, 1914 which went to press while its editor was in prison, hunger- and thirst-striking, before her release on June 18.

176

remarkable effect on Mr. Asquith's mind", as "it seemed that he had not previously realised that many women work for their living."[6] Emmeline Pethick Lawrence was later to observe that the Premier's capitulation was "the first sign" that he was "beginning to change his attitude of hostility to woman's suffrage".[7]

The significance of this event also struck George Dangerfield, an historian of this period, who observes in a memorable passage that it was "one of the more important moments in English history" and a "scene that deserves to be recorded on a canvas":

> The late summer evening drifts out of Parliament Square.... A momentary gleam, perhaps, could be made to light upon that little group of people, as they bend over the recumbent Sylvia with expressions of solicitude and agitation and triumph ... the artist might depict, upon the faces of the police, some mingling traces of admiration and shame, and for his necessary touch of historical irony he would suggest in the background the dust draped statue of Oliver Cromwell.
>
> Oh, yes, the scene is important enough. *We are winning!*[1] That shrill cry in Parliament Square had a deep significance. Nor is it only the significance which attached to every movement of the militant Suffragettes: the significance, that is, of a new life in the soul of women. It is curiously enough the small voice of all England in its last year before the war. The only question one has to inquire into is whether anyone heard it correctly.[8]

The struggle for votes for women, as my mother was later to write, became "more and more arduous" in 1914. Then, when she and most other Suffragettes felt they were "on the eve of success",[9] the First World War broke out. Hardships and sorrow descended on the East End. Husbands and sons were called up, meagre separation allowances were slow to arrive. Factories closed down, prices soared, families became destitute. Mothers, she later wrote in an autobiographical passage, "came to me with their wasted little ones. I saw starvation look at me from patient eyes. I knew then that I should never return to my art."[10]

There was indeed almost an inevitability about it, for, as Emmeline Pethick Lawrence was later to observe, Sylvia's "passion for beauty, great as it was, had to yield in the end to her passion of imaginative pity. She entered into the humiliations and sufferings of the great company of over-worked and poverty-stricken people, especially of over-worked mothers."[11]

In the months and years which followed, the erstwhile artist and her East End comrades continued the struggle for the vote, but also worked to ameliorate the economic conditions of the poor. She sought to obtain official relief where it could be obtained, and where this was not possible appealed to the public. She established a toy factory to create work, as well as several unemployment and distress bureaux, cost price restaurants, mother and infant centres, and so on.

Immersed in such matters, bound by the routine of bringing out a weekly newspaper (which she was to continue for a full ten years), and living in the bleak and grimy slums which she had always so hated, she had no time, indeed scarcely any real inclination, to devote to her paint brush. "I found so much distress among the women around me in the East End of London," she was afterwards to write, "that I felt I had to do what I could to help them, and that I could not yet return to my beloved profession."[12]

It was significant of her involvement in the East End that the *Dreadnought* – and a short-lived cultural review called *Germinal* which she edited in 1923–4 – were illustrated not by her but by others. In both journals she published works by Walter Crane whom she had always admired, and who also sent her some of his drawings to be used as designs for toys made in the cooperative factory.

Two younger artists also contributed freely to the *Dreadnought*. One of them, Herbert Cole, was, like her, a former student of the Manchester School of Art who had been influenced, as she had, by Walter Crane, and other Pre-Raphaelites, William Morris, Holman Hunt and the Manchester artist Frederick Shields. Cole, who had begun his career in the service of a Manchester building contractor for whom he produced saints and angels for church walls and cartoons for stained glass, was later employed on the *Pall Mall Magazine*, and achieved fame as the illustrator of *Gulliver's Travels*, *The Ancient Mariner* and other works.[13]

The other artist who drew for her was Amy Browning, her old fellow student at the Royal College of Art and principal aide on the Prince's Skating Rink murals. She helped in producing designs for the toy factory, and went down to the East End on Saturday afternoons to teach drawing to any of the workers who cared to learn, either to improve their toymaking skills or for their own pleasure.[14]

Though Sylvia had herself ceased to draw, the works of these two artists, at this time largely satirical, anti-militarist and anti-capitalist in tone, would seem to reflect her artistic traditions and taste, as well as her political preoccupations at this time, and symbolise her deliberate abandonment of art.

✥ 12 The First World War; the Rise of Fascism; Author and Mother; the Italo-Ethiopian War; Emigration to Addis Ababa

THE REST OF MY MOTHER'S LIFE lies outside the field of art – and hence must be considered a postscript to the present volume. Though she had irrevocably abandoned her cherished profession as an artist she was significantly influenced by her student days in Italy, as well as by the Suffragette movement and the poverty and political activity in the East End of London which had combined to drag her from her easel and brush.

Her artistic and humanitarian convictions, and her life in the East End, made her, like many of the Socialists of her generation, a pacifist, and as such a strong opponent of the First World War. Though more concerned with alleviating the distress caused by the conflagration than actually working against hostilities as such, she was convicted of addressing an anti-war meeting. She did not go to prison as on previous occasions, for a group of Derbyshire miners paid the fine for her. In her attitude to the conflict she differed, as earlier over the more extreme tactics of Suffragette militancy, from her mother and sister Christabel, both of whom were enthusiastic supporters of the Allied cause, so much so indeed that, as is well known, they suspended their agitation for the vote "until the war was won". Sylvia and her East End movement, on the contrary, continued throughout this time to demand the immediate enfranchisement of women.*

---

* Women's participation in the war, the disappearance from the political scene of some of the principal opponents of votes for women, and fears of a return of Suffragette militancy, all contributed to the Government's decision, in 1917, to grant limited enfranchisement of women. A Bill giving the vote to women over thirty years of age who were occupiers, or wives of occupiers, of land or property of not less than five pounds annual value, and to women over thirty who held university degrees, passed the third reading in the House of Commons on December 7, 1917. It did, not, however, reach the statute book until November 21, 1918, ten days after the Armistice, and within three weeks of a long-delayed general election.

Complete equality in voting rights between the sexes was delayed for a full decade, until 1928. When it came, this long-needed reform created little excitement; the principle of women's enfranchisement for which the Suffragettes and others had fought for so long had by then been accepted by all but the most diehard of anti-suffragists.

Leaving Holloway Prison, May 1921.
PHOTO: RADIO TIMES HULTON PICTURE LIBRARY

Towards the end of the war she became a passionate supporter of the Bolshevik Revolution in Russia, and a no less committed opponent of Allied intervention against it. In this respect too, her stance was entirely the opposite of that of her mother who had earlier gone to Russia, under the British government's auspices, to urge the then Russian leader Kerensky, to continue the struggle against the Kaiser. My mother, who in July 1917 had changed the name of her weekly newspaper, the *Woman's Dreadnought*, to that of the *Worker's Dreadnought*, proceeded to found a People's Russian Information Bureau, and organised a "Hands off Russia" campaign. A pamphlet of hers on the Allied "conspiracy" against Soviet Russia was published in Petrograd (later Leningrad) in French and German in 1919–20. All this caused some of the East Enders less interested in world affairs to nickname her "Little Miss Russia". In 1920 she travelled illegally by way of Murmansk to Moscow – a journey fraught with many difficulties which she later described in a book entitled *Soviet Russia as I Saw It* (which appeared in 1921). While in Russia she attended the first congress of the Third International, and conversed with Lenin who later criticised her in his polemic *Left-Wing Communism: An Infantile*

Disorder. On her return to Britain she was imprisoned, for the last time, under the Defence of the Realm Act.

Sentenced on that occasion to six months in gaol she decided, much to the dismay of the prison parson who still regarded the "Huns" with passionate war-time dislike, to study German, and added to her earlier prison diet of the Bible, Karl Marx's *Das Kapital* which she read in the original. The lengthy, and at times seemingly repetitious, discussion of surplus value struck her as tedious, but excellent for learning the German language.

After her release she published a slim volume, *Writ on Cold Slate*. Unpolished and at times poorly scanned, as she was well aware,* the poems are nevertheless interesting, both autobiographically and for the light they throw on conditions in Holloway Prison. The significance of the title is apparent from the opening stanzas which bemoan the prisoner's lack of writing material. They declare that in the past poets had immortalised their love in verse while prisoners had used writing materials provided by their jailers, but:

> *Only this age that loudly boasts Reform,*
> *hath set its seal of vengeance 'gainst the mind,*
> *decreeing nought in prison shall be writ,*
> *save on cold slate, and swiftly washed away.*

Most of the poems speak of prison life. One verse tells of the author's arrival in gaol, brought there in a Black Maria, the cold and dreariness of the prison cell, and the sense of isolation when "clanged the heavy door and double locked".

Sense of confinement is likewise expressed in "Morn" which refers to the cell window as a "cruel white dazzling square" that "first aroused mine eyes reluctant from their slumbers". Turning to the small birds which flew freely in the sky – like symbols of freedom – she cries out:

> *Sing, sing, my little songsters, sing and sing;*
> *twitter your lively twitterings …*
> *carry our minds away with ye from here.*

Elaborating on this theme she continues:

> *Sharp beats beside me the retreating wing*
> *of brother pigeon at the window-sill;*
> *from bread I lay for him he nervous starts,*
> *lest he, detained, be captive held like me.*

---

* Copies in my possession are full of revisions in my mother's hand.

Another poem "Unto the Birds", contains the lines:

> for all the birds are singing to their loves,
> and every note finds echo here within
> where loving hearts their parted loves desire,
> mourning the smart of absence long endured.
>
> Behind these bars the eager blood doth rise,
> then falleth down, then sadly falleth down,
> for we in love captivity must lie
> and night long weep the slow unheeded tears.

The theme of incarceration found expression again in a poem on the clouds:

> O clouds that drift across the sky
> take with ye now mine active brain
> that would not be confined.
>
> Most wondrous are your myriad shapes
> and lovely are your colours fair,
> but marrèd by these bars.
>
> Could I but range now, far and free
> on some swift plane I'd follow ye,
> and leave the cell behind.
>
> O skies that bring the sun and showers
> and little birds a chirping
> Ye all do set me weeping,
> that I'm a prisoner still.

Other aspects of prison life, including the monotonous toil to which she, like other women at Holloway, was subjected, are described in "The Cleaners":

> Daily we cleaners, ere the earliest dawn,
> drag weary limbs from bed; and I must haste,
> haste to the cleaning of full fifteen cells,
> and two long corridors must also scrub
> before the great ones come, swift marching through;
> and as I scrub they call me "Cleaner! Here!"
>
> Their orders all conflict, I'm still in fault,
> and ever driven, though I pant with haste,
> whilst every minute finds some further task,
> till limbs are all a-tumble, head awhirl.
>
> Windows to clean, and so they push me in;
> something is spilt, a cleaner must clean up,
> or coals to carry; so I stagger off,

bending my back under too heavy loads,
for I must strain, although her hands are free:
the officer who guards me as I go.

Our food is scant; our beds too hard to sleep;
but we're in prison, we are cleaners here.

Many of her poems are devoted to individual prisoners, common female criminals, as the law regarded them, with whom she shared her detention. These verses reveal her interest in and compassion for the inmates, and her feeling of involvement in their lives and problems. One such poem tells of an aged woman in the exercise yard. Entitled "What's She, the Old Soul with the Demented Looks", it declares:

What's she, the old soul with wild crispish hair
and black eyes burning in a pallid face,
her fingers sticking out like waxen spikes
'neath the long sleeves that half her hands engulf
and shoes for lack of laces, white lint ties?

Goes she not tamed among the ordered file,
but hither, thither, runneth o'er the grass
gathers green leaves and tells a chattering tale,
her garments flapping in the frisky wind,
her stockings and her garters round her feet.

Now stern the officer to order calls,
pays she no heed, but eager rusheth on,
to pick a crust from some cell window cast,
and, childish, fancying pigeons to entice,
chases their buoyant flight with tottering tread.

The well-fed magistrate hath felt no shame
to send this old demented granny here.

Sympathy for a fellow prisoner is likewise apparent in another poem:

After three years the maiden will be free;
no fear restrains her, no, no padded cell.

She sings through lagging days, heedless of blame,
in rhymes of impromptu jeers at prison life.

A pauper child, some paltry gawds she stole,
therefore was she in budding youth hid here;
her limbs, their childish lankiness o'erpast,
growing in roundness fair for love's caress,
her heart that did begin to know swift beats,

her waking womb that now desired to mate,
her laughter ringing, springing like a fount
of sparkling water flashing in the sun,
her voice a-lilting gay, her dancing feet:
all harsh subdued and shut away in cell.

Telling of the eventual release from prison of this "homeless child", and of her subsequent entry into "some hostel for fallen girls", the poem asks:

Where will thy wanderings lead thee, maiden frail,
in this cruel, cunning world to thee so strange,
to thee, grown simple from long bridling here?

The social comment implicit in the above two poems is evident also in "Mary", a verse about an old prostitute:

They named thee prostitute and sent thee here,
poor ancient Mary, with thy parchment-face,
with mumbling chin approaching to the nose,
a-drooping pinched o'er toothless gums indrawn.

Someone who loves thee came so far today
to see thee in a cage and comfort bring,
and now thou'rt painful hobbling back to cell;
bent on thy stick, with wardress aid beside.

'Tis all too much for thy frost-bitten feet,
frozen past cure those icy winter nights
when for a bed thou on doorsteps didst couch.

Begging's out-dated, all policemen know it;
soliciting's the sin the Bench would scourge;
So, Mary, thou'rt called whore to suit the fashion.

The silly bait was swallowed by the "Beak";
as thou lack'st coppers, so he lacketh sense.[1]

She was later disillusioned with what she considered the autocratic and anti-humanitarian aspects of the Communist movement. During Stalin's time she spoke with horror of the purges, and particularly of the trial of Bukharin and other old Bolsheviks, several of whom she had met in Moscow a decade or so earlier, and in whose alleged self-confessed treason she found it impossible to believe.

Her interest in Italy which had begun with her study in Venice early in the century, and was intensified by later visits to that country, in particular when she attended the Socialist Congress at Bologna in September 1919, made her a bitter opponent of Mussolini who came to power in 1922. Her awareness, and hatred, of Fascism was no doubt reinforced by her friendship with my father, Silvio Erasmus Corio, an Italian libertarian Socialist from Saluzzo near Turin. He collaborated with her in a number of journalistic, publishing and printing activities, and helped to bring out the *Dreadnought* during her absence in Russia and in prison. His name appears as the printer of several of her publications.

After the rise of Mussolini she initiated two anti-Fascist organisations in Britain, the Society of Friends of Italian Freedom, and the Women's International Matteotti Committee – named after the Italian Socialist parliamentarian murdered on the dictator's orders in 1923. She was the honorary secretary of the latter body, and was, as we shall see, to remain a strong antagonist of Fascism throughout the years ahead.

In 1924 she at last gave up editing the *Dreadnought,* and moved out of London with my father. Like many East Enders they settled in more or less the nearest stretch of countryside beyond it – in Woodford Green, Essex. Their first home was the Red Cottage, an old rambling single-storey structure on the High Road, where she had earlier purchased a piece of land, and where they ran a tea shop,* after which they moved to a somewhat more commodious three-floor building at 3 Charteris Road. (It was in Woodford that I was to spend my infancy and childhood.)

My mother, freed at last from the chore of bringing out a weekly newspaper, devoted the next decade or so to the writing of books, as well as – to "keep the wolf from the door" – articles for other people's journals. It was not long before a spate of volumes, as well as innumerable articles on a wide variety of subjects poured forth from her pen.

Keenly interested in types of social organisation different from those in western Europe she turned first, surprisingly enough, to India. (Her study in Woodford which was lined with books on all sides from floor to ceiling was, I recall, full of books on India.) She wrote a six-hundred-page volume *India and the Earthly Paradise* which was published in Bombay in 1926. This work, which is scarcely known in Europe, was highly critical of the caste system, the depressed status of the "untouchables" and various aspects of Indian superstition. Though supporting the idea of independence, "as a necessary step in

---

* Though my mother later sold the property, an anti-war monument which she had erected there in 1934 is still in existence. Sculpted in the form of a bomb, it is dedicated, ironically, to the British statesmen "who in 1933 upheld the right to use bombing planes" to keep the frontier tribesmen in India in order. The monument was defaced several times by local Fascists.

the evolution of the peoples of India, and one which leaves them more free than now to unravel their own problems", she warned that "the expulsion of foreign exploitation" could simply mean "the growth of native exploitation". The book incurred the wrath of several orthodox Brahmins, and was as a result scarcely distributed.

Long convinced of the need for closer contacts between the nations of the world, and assuming, like so many of her generation, that this would foster world peace, at about this time she began a study of international languages. In 1927 she gave a lecture to the annual conference of the Société Internationale de Philologie, Sciences, et Beaux Arts, in London, on the theme "Is an International Language Possible ?" In the same year she wrote a book entitled *Delphos: The Future of International Language*. It came out in favour of Interlingua, or Latin without inflexions, a language which had been devised by Professor Peano. She argued that it was more "natural" than Esperanto which was an artificial mixture of entirely unrelated tongues.

Shortly afterwards, herself by then a mother – I, her only child, had been born in December 1927 when she was already forty-five years of age – she embarked on a review of maternity conditions in Britain. She was struck, like the early social scientists of the previous century, by the discrepancy of infant and maternal mortality between rich and poor. Her findings appeared, in 1930, in a book with the provocative title and sub-title: *Save the Mothers: A Plea for Measures to Prevent the Annual Loss of about 3,000 Child-bearing Mothers and 2,000 Infant Lives in England and Wales and a Similar Grievous Wastage in Other Countries*. This work, attracting some attention in English-speaking countries, was shortly afterwards translated into Japanese. The Tokyo edition had a frontispiece of the author and her three-year-old baby son, both with a hint of Japanese features.

Meanwhile, having been interested in folk-art since her student days – particularly that of Romania which seemed to her specially fine – and being by then more involved in writing than in art, she made a study of Romanian authors. Greatly impressed with such works of the national poet Eminescu as were then available in French, Italian and German, she decided to translate some of his verse into English. She was assisted in this by a Romanian in London, Dr. Stefanovici, who provided her with a rough English text, after which by poring over a dictionary she learned a good bit of the language, and was able to put the translation into the original Romanian metres. There resulted from this cooperation the *Poems of Mihail Eminescu,* published in 1930, which had an introduction by the renowned Romanian scholar N.Iorga

Sylvia Pankhurst, a studio portrait, 1930.

A portrait based on the opposite photograph drawn in 1953 by Sylvia's old college friend Austin Osman Spare.

PHOTO: IVY TIMS

(who was later to be killed by the Romanian Fascist Iron Guard). There was also a preface by Bernard Shaw who, apparently assuming that the work was her own and not in fact a translation, commented that she was "the queerest idiot-genius of this age".

Perhaps the most significant poem in the volume, certainly one of her favourites, was "Emperor and Proletarian", a long piece which emphasises the essential equality of mankind irrespective of social class, and is full of allusion to France around the time of the Paris Commune. The opening stanza speaks of the conditions of the nineteenth-century poor and underprivileged, after which the Romanian poet, addressing the masses on their political and social oppression, and on the inequality of the law which was operated by and for the rich, declares:

What's justice? See the mighty, behind their fortune's shielding,
Erect their laws and edicts, to serve them as a foil. . . .
And hold in subjugation your lives of ceaseless toil.

The poet, voicing the discontent of the French, proceeds to give vent to a call for rebellion:

> *Crush down the social order, accursèd and unfair,*
> *That 'twixt the poor and wealthy our human kind divides.*

He then conjures up the picture of Napoleon III in Paris, on the eve of his deposition:

> *Beside the old Seine's waters, with pallid looks and sombrous,*
> *In coach of gala splendour, the mighty Caesar passed.*

Before long, however, the mock Bonapartist empire has crumbled, the French dictator has found refuge across the channel in Britain and:

> *Paris in flames is seething....*
> *And towers, like inky torches, flare crashing to their doom.*
> *An epoch on its death-bed, with Paris for its tomb.*[2]

A poem in a different style and mood was "Why comest not? Why comest not?" – a lover's lament set in the autumn countryside of Romania. The first verse declares:

> *Behold the swallows quit the eaves,*
> *And fall the yellowed walnut leaves,*
> *The hoar frost doth the vineyard rot;*
> *Why comest not? Why comest not?*

My mother shortly afterwards completed perhaps her most important work, *The Suffragette Movement*, which was published in 1931 with the subtitle *An Intimate Account of Persons and Ideals*. A history with a major autobiographical content, it was dedicated to me. (As a child of four I was scarcely aware of the fact, though it fell to me almost half a century later to write a brief introduction for it when reprinted by Virago in 1977.)

Her next book, which appeared in 1932, was *The Home Front*. Described in the subtitle as *A Mirror to Life in England during the World War*, it tells, *inter alia*, of its author's activities in the East End, and was dedicated to her old Suffragette comrade Emmeline Pethick Lawrence, with whom she saw eye to eye on many political and social questions. The two women, both veterans of the Suffragette movement though each had differed from the official WSPU leadership on issues of substance, were to remain warm friends for the rest of their lives. (My mother often went down to the Pethick Lawrences' home in Peaslake, Surrey, where I heard her and Emmeline share reminiscences about old times. My mother would also speak of the political activities in which she

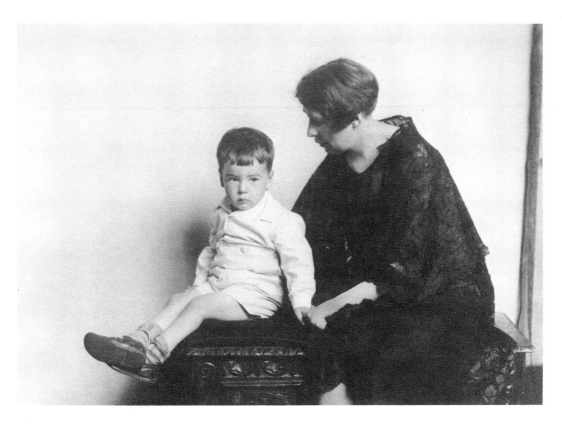

Above: Sylvia with her son Richard.

Left: Sylvia in Romania, by the
statue of the poet Eminescu,
overlooking the Black Sea.
PHOTO: A. PETRESCU

was then engaged and the two also wrote to each other frequently.

While writing these books my mother continued her anti-Fascist activities, and in November 1932 brought out the first, and only, issue of a newspaper entitled *Humanity*. Described as the organ of the "Women's International Matteotti Committee" it bore the slogans: "You have made of your prisons a temple of honour" – W.E.Gladstone, and "You can kill me but you cannot kill the thoughts within me" – Giacomo Matteotti. The paper published messages of support from such British women Socialists as Jenny Lee, Ethel Manin and Frida Laski, as well as Bertrand Russell's wife Dora Russell and the Italian anti-Fascists Professor Salvemini and Pietro Nenni.

My mother and other translators of Eminescu were shortly afterwards officially invited to Romania for the unveiling in 1934 of the poet's monument in Constanza overlooking the Black Sea. Having by then completed *The Suffragette Movement* and *The Home Front* she was, I remember, in a relaxed mood, and taking my father and me with her, travelled across Europe by train. We avoided Italy, where my father would have been arrested, but passed through Nazi Germany. That night the police, while making a routine search of the train, noticed that my parents had placed a page of the London *Times* over part of the lamp in our compartment to allow me to sleep; the paper was promptly confiscated. We spent a few hours in Berlin then be-draped in black-lined Nazi flags for Hindenburg's funeral. It did not escape her attention that when we went to the greengrocers to purchase some fruit for the journey, though my father paid, the shopkeeper handed her the bag to carry.

She fell in love with Romania, its beautiful countryside and fine peasant costumes, and spent many happy days admiring the Byzantine-style paintings on its medieval churches. (As a child I found these inspections in the summer heat almost unending and though naturally impressed by the beautiful church of Curtea de Arges with its richly coloured twisted domes, was more amused, I fear, by the even more colourful uniforms of King Carol's palace guards, the hues of which seemed to change each day.)

While in Romania she made many friends and met a number of artists, among them a woman who during the war had been obliged to produce her own paints out of flowers, leaves and divers types of earth. My mother began writing a book on the country, but because of the outbreak of the Ethiopian war shortly afterwards lacked the time to complete the historical chapters she had wished to include and therefore left the work unfinished.*

---

* After her death I deposited the text, together with much of her other writings, in the International Institute of Social History in Amsterdam.

She also at about this time embarked on a study of the international Socialist and Communist movement based partially on her own reminiscences, to be entitled *In the Red Twilight*. This too she was obliged to leave unpublished as she had not the time to complete the research she thought necessary for the work.* Her writings, like her paintings, were the result of much toil and effort, and her books usually involved considerable research.

The last of this series of published writings was, perhaps aptly, a short biography of her mother – with whom she had differed politically on several deeply felt issues** – *The Life of Emmeline Pankhurst*. It appeared in 1936 with the sub-title *The Suffragette Struggle for Women's Citizenship*.

As a mother she was also interested in children's stories, and contemplated writing a book based on tales she and I told each other on the way to or from school – to which, though always busy writing, speaking or organising, she escorted me regularly for several years. The story was to be called *Dogland*, but for lack of a publisher never got beyond the first sixty-two pages and a concluding synopsis. The principal characters were Jack, a big Airedale (a breed of dog we always kept in those days), and Rip, a beautiful young deerhound, who in the opening paragraph are seen at play. They were so wild that "they trampled down plants, smashed flower pots, overturned ladders and tore the washing from the clothes line."

The last quarter of my mother's life, the only part I remember personally (and therefore touch upon in somewhat greater detail), was much influenced by the Fascist aggression of the 1930s and its consequences. Having been opposed to the Italian dictatorship since its inception, and seeing its militarist and expansionist character, she felt sure that Mussolini would sooner or later embark on a policy of conquest. The pretext for the first Fascist war – against Ethiopia,

---

* This volume is deposited in the Institute of Social History in Amsterdam.

** Emmeline Pankhurst became a Conservative parliamentary candidate and died in 1928.

On learning at the close of 1927 of her mother's decision to stand as a Conservative candidate, my mother wrote to the Socialist journal *Forward* to express her "profound grief that Emmeline Pankhurst should have deserted the old cause of progress". Stating her own humanitarian Socialist position, she continued: "For my part I rejoice in having enlisted for life in the socialist movement, in which the work of Owen, Marx, Kropotkin, William Morris and Keir Hardie, and such pioneering efforts as those of my father, Richard Marsden Pankhurst, both before and during the rise of the movement in this country, are an enduring memory. It is naturally most painful to me to write this, but I feel it incumbent upon me, in view of this defection, to reaffirm my faith in the cause of social and international fraternity, and to utter a word of sorrow that one who in the past has rendered such service should now, with that sad pessimism which sometimes comes with advancing years, and may result from too strenuous effort, join the reaction. . . ."

then better known in Europe as Abyssinia – was the Wal Wal incident of December 1934, when Italian forces probing far across the frontiers of the Italian Somaliland colony clashed with Ethiopian troops. She believed, rightly as it turned out, that Mussolini would seize the occasion to launch a war of aggression. Though she had never visited the far off country, then virtually the only indigenous independent state on the African continent, she was, as an artist, already familiar with its remarkable processional crosses taken during a British expedition against Emperor Theodore in 1868, which were on permanent display in the British Museum.[3] She had also heard something about Ethiopia's ancient civilisation from my father who, then himself a conscript in the Italian army, had met Italian soldiers returning home after capture by Emperor Menelik at the close of an earlier Italian invasion of that country in 1896.

Within days of Wal Wal, she was writing to British newspapers to argue that the incident should be regarded as a matter of grave concern, liable if neglected to result in a major breach of international peace. She subsequently approached the Ethiopian legation in London, and found that the minister, Charles Workneh Martin, an Ethiopian medical doctor trained in India and Britain, was short of staff and funds, and in no position to match the flood of propaganda produced by the protagonists of Fascist Italy. Much impressed by his obvious integrity and lack of political guile, as well as by the difficulties he was encountering in bringing up his family in a foreign land, she offered to help him.

In October 1935 the long expected Fascist invasion of Ethiopia actually began – without in fact any declaration of war – when Fascist armies crossed the frontier of Ethiopia from the neighbouring Italian colonies of Eritrea in the north and Somalia in the south. My mother was one of those who helped to rally British public opinion in support of the victim of aggression,[4] and in the demand that League of Nations' sanctions be invoked in its defence. She was a founder member of the Abyssinia Association, a society set up in Britain to work for the Ethiopian cause. As the invaders advanced on the Ethiopian capital, Addis Ababa, in April 1936, she decided that there was a need to establish a newspaper to state the Ethiopian case and to keep interest in it alive after the novelty waned, and public opinion, so often fickle, became engrossed in other matters. She chose for her publication the name *Ethiopia News,* but, seeking also a wider forum, added before it the words *New Times* which she thought would have appeal because of the association with Charlie Chaplin's then much spoken of film, *Modern Times.* Though not a particularly gregarious person, she was still in contact with numerous friends who had worked with her in the Suffragette movement or in the East End, and was in close contact with others in various anti-Fascist organisations. Many such people became readers and contributors of the paper.

The first issue of *New Times and Ethiopia News* was printed on May 5, 1936, my mother's fifty-fourth birthday, and, by coincidence, the day the Italian troops marched in to Addis Ababa. In her first editorial she wrote:

> *New Times and Ethiopia News* appears at the moment when the fortunes of Ethiopia seem at their lowest ebb; the greater the need for an advocate and friend.
>
> We know that the difficulties facing her are grave, but we do not falter, either in faith or determination that they shall be overcome.
>
> The cause of Ethiopia cannot be divided from the cause of international justice, which is permanent, and is not to be determined by ephemeral military victories.

Outlining the policy which the paper was to follow in the years ahead she continued:

> We shall set ourselves resolutely to combat Fascist propaganda, to secure the continuance and strengthening of sanctions. . . . We shall strive to induce measures by the League to resist Fascist usurpation and defend Ethiopia, and will persistently urge that Britain take the responsibility of initiating an active League policy on these lines. . . .
>
> We shall urge, in season and out, that the facts of the Italo-Ethiopian war and the reason of League intervention therein be broadcast in all languages to inform all people thereon, and especially those of Italy where free information is denied.
>
> *New Times* is opposed to the conception of dictatorship. It understands that Fascism destroys all personal liberty. . . .
>
> We draw a profound distinction between the Italian Fascist government and the Italian people, who are enslaved today, but whose freedom is slowly but surely being prepared by the martyrdom of thousands of heroic men and women. . . .

In the following month the Ethiopian Emperor Haile Selassie arrived in London, and she was one of the crowd that thronged the station to greet him. She met him later on many occasions, several of them in Bath where he spent the greater part of his exile. At this first encounter she told him frankly as a Republican that she supported him not because he was an emperor, but because she believed his cause, the cause of Ethiopia, was a just one. She subsequently interviewed him formally for her paper and got him to talk about the reforms he had introduced in his country before the war. (Thirty years later, meeting me by chance in the University in Addis Ababa some years after her death, he was to speak to me of her as a remarkable woman, and when I mentioned to

With Emperor Haile
Selassie in Bath – a
photograph taken by
the author as a child.

him that I was writing a history of Ethiopia he interrupted me to say I should
instead write her biography.)

Her work in relation to Ethiopia, and to a lesser extent other victim
nations, was to absorb her for much longer than she or anyone else might have
anticipated in 1936. Having begun by organising meetings, and speaking and
writing in favour of the strengthening of League of Nations sanctions against
the aggressor, she was soon involved in efforts to reveal the extent of Fascist
war atrocities in Ethiopia, including the bombing of Red Cross hospitals and
ambulances, and the use of mustard gas which Italian propagandists sought to
deny. She was one of those who urged the need for an international loan for
Ethiopia to enable its government to continue the war. She travelled to the
League of Nations in Geneva to report on the discussion about Ethiopia and
helped lobby delegates and on returning to Britain was active in many ways in
assisting Ethiopian refugees who had escaped to neighbouring countries as well
as answering and rebutting Fascist propaganda. After the collapse of the
Emperor's armies in the spring of 1936 and the Italian capture of Addis Ababa
in May, the League soon called off sanctions, but many Ethiopians refused to
give up the struggle. Sizeable groups of Ethiopian patriots, largely unknown to
the outside world, began to carry out guerilla resistance, and it became the

raison d'être of *New Times and Ethiopia News* to publicise their struggle, to prevent British, and as far as possible, world opinion from forgetting the remote African country, many of whose sons and daughters had refused to bow before the Fascist dictator. It was not long before special issues of her newspaper, translated into the Ethiopian language Amharic, were being smuggled into the still only nominally occupied country.

New Times and Ethiopia News was run, edited, and despatched by a team of young girls in Charteris Road, Woodford, and was printed a few miles away in Walthamstow where my father travelled one or two days a week to work with the printers "on the stone" before "putting it to bed". The paper carried long serialised articles by its editor on such topics as "Fascism as It Is", and "How Hitler Rose to Power", as well as lengthy leaders which, as I well recall, often kept her up all night. Other articles were written by the Ethiopian minister, Dr. Martin, British scholars like Professor F.L.Lucas and Professor Beridale Keith, the sometime Ethiopian correspondent of *The Times*, George L.Steer, the internationalist W.Arnold-Forster MP, Captain Arnold Weinholt of Australia, the French feminist Andrée Forny, the Belgian senator Henri Rolin and a Dutch clergyman Dr. J.B.T.Hugenholz who ran a pro-Ethiopian organisation in Holland. Other contributors included several Italian refugees such as the author Professor Gaetano Salvemini, an exile in the United States, Professor Francesco Frola in Mexico, and Francesco Nitti who had fought against Mussolini in the Spanish civil war, as well as the Spanish Republican Louis Aragistan, the Hungarian refugee Bela Menczer and the Romanian D. Dem Dimancescu. There were likewise articles by Dr. Harold A. Moody, founder of the League of Coloured Peoples, and, in later years, the South African novelist Peter Abrahams.

The newspaper necessitated a considerable amount of fund-raising, by bazaars, garden fêtes and the like, and was distributed free of charge to all Members of Parliament – on special occasions being posted "to be delivered in the House" – as well as to influential or supposedly influential persons throughout the world. Efforts were also made to have the paper on sale at all by-election meetings where the British government's policy of appeasement was often under attack.

The publication achieved a notable circulation in English-speaking Africa, and among blacks in the United States, as well as in the West Indies, where a series of articles entitled "Africans to Africans" created much interest. Numerous articles were lifted, with or without acknowledgment, by the African Press, thereby contributing significantly to the growing tide of pan-Africanism. My mother was in contact with many of the African nationalists of the period, particularly those in England, such as Jomo Kenyatta, Wallace Johnston, George Padmore, T.R.Makonnen and others who came to the house, which (like that of her father before her) was visited by people of many nationalities fighting for their emancipation and whose cause she endeavoured to assist.[5] She also exchanged *New Times and Ethiopia News* with numerous African newspapers, such as the *West African Pilot* and the *Comet,* as well as black publications in the United States, like the *Chicago Defender,* and corresponded with the great black scholar W. E. B. Dubois and others. (She was later to speak with appreciation of the extent to which the Ethiopian war had assisted the breaking-down of parochialism in Africa and the emergence of wider pan-African thought.)

She was also in close contact with many Italian anti-Fascists, among them several who had dramatically escaped from the penal island for political prisoners, in a fast motor-boat, piercing their used petrol tanks each time they threw one overboard to prevent it serving as a marker for their pursuers. Among those who visited her in Woodford was Carlo Rosselli, editor in Paris of the anti-Fascist journal *Giustizia e Libertà* who was later assassinated on Mussolini's orders (after which *New Times and Ethiopia News* often reproduced, and later incorporated in its title design his emblem of a flaming sword of justice.) Other visitors included the Treves brothers who left Italy relatively late because of the enactment of Mussolini's racial laws; and Recchioni, the editor of the Anarchist weekly, *Freedom,* and his vivacious companion, Marie Louise Berneri, author of *Journey Through Utopia.*

My mother's espousal of the Ethiopian, and generally anti-Fascist cause was not unknown to Mussolini, who, himself something of a journalist, attacked her in more than one of his articles which were always italicised in the Italian Press.

The paper, and its editor, also rallied to the cause of the Spanish Republican government, then engaged in mortal struggle with Franco, and sought to expose Falangist atrocities, for example, at Guernica, as well as the extent of Italian and German involvement in the Spanish Civil War. Many articles were likewise devoted to Japanese aggression in China, the plight of the Jews and others in Hitler's Reich – and the misdeeds of Stalin in relation to the old Bolsheviks and others, as well as later to the iniquity, as she regarded it, of the Nazi-Soviet pact signed by Ribbentrop and Molotov in 1939.

My mother, always a quiet, gentle and soft-spoken, if determined person – in all these respects not dissimilar from her own mother – was throughout this

PLATE XIII WSPU membership card.

Opposite: PLATE XIV **A Study.**

PLATE XV Untitled. Portrait drawing of a young woman.

PLATE XVI Untitled. A landscape showing rolling hills descending toward the sea.

time organising and addressing meetings and conferences on Ethiopian matters. She wrote innumerable letters, and urged others to write, to the national press, as well as to MPs, cabinet ministers, foreign statesmen – among them President and Mrs. Roosevelt whose country – like the USSR – never recognised the Italian conquest. Her letters were most frequently published in the *Manchester Guardian,* which on occasion supported her in its leading articles, and such Liberal and Labour newspapers as the *News Chronicle* and the *Daily Herald.* She likewise produced articles for *Picture Post.*

She was also engaged in a variety of other humanitarian and anti-Fascist activities, such as working against the deportation of refugees who had arrived in Britain,* finding jobs for Jewish refugees and homes for Basque children, distributing pamphlets on rice-paper for circulation in Italy and the Italian colonies,** and despatching surgical instruments† to one of the Italian penal islands for the use of political prisoners.

The Ethiopian struggle, contrary to what some may suppose, was moreover constantly posing new problems. Correspondents in the French Somali port of Jibuti and elsewhere sent regular news of patriot resistance, including major Ethiopian victories over the enemy, while several of the Emperor's emissaries succeeded in touring the large areas of the country which had not submitted to the invader, and returned with information on the people's determination to continue the struggle. News was also received, through various channels, of the Addis Ababa massacre of February 1937 which followed an attempt by two Eritreans on the life of the Italian viceroy, Graziani. Two of Dr. Martin's sons were among those murdered. Such reports were publicised and siphoned to the world Press to keep interest in Ethiopia, the first victim of Fascist aggression, alive. All sorts of questions relating to the country were moreover constantly erupting. The Italian government having announced its "conquests" proceeded for example to lay claim to Ethiopian state properties

---

* When a refugee was faced with deportation a Member of Parliament would be persuaded to raise the matter with the Home Office, thus automatically producing a stay of deportation while the matter was being examined and later explained to the MP. If the government remained adamant in its decision to deport, a second and, if necessary, a succession of members had to be approached so that the case could be prolonged for many months.

** During the period of League of Nations' sanctions against Italy one consignment of this literature, which was printed in Paris, was seized by officious British customs officers in the belief that it was an Italian export; it took weeks of correspondence before it was released.

† This equipment, shiny and laid out in its cases in neat rows prior to its despatch, fascinated me when I saw it as a child, but was soon seized by the Fascist prison authorities.

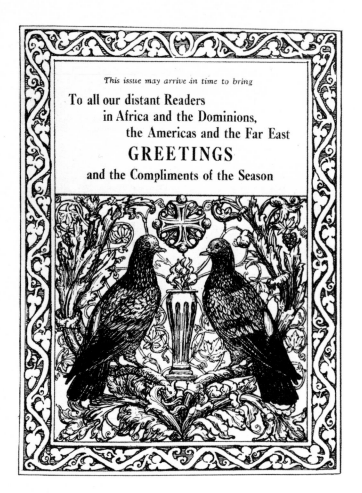

No. 90: Sylvia's last
decorative effort: the
cover of a programme
for an Ethiopian fund-
raising gathering, also
used to send greetings to
the readers of her
newspaper *New Times
and Ethiopia News*, on
December 17, 1938.

abroad. This was stoutly contested by Haile Selassie, and the matter came
before British courts of justice in a series of cases which, despite the activities of
the pro-Ethiopian lobby, were decided in favour of the invader.[6] Later, in 1938,
the British government, notwithstanding the opposition of the Abyssinia
Association, *New Times and Ethiopia News* and others, gave formal
recognition to Mussolini's ill-gotten empire.[7]

The Ethiopian cause and the editing of *New Times and Ethiopia News*,
like her work in the East End and the running of the *Dreadnought* in former
days, occupied every moment, leaving Sylvia neither time nor thoughts for art.
In the autumn of 1938, while preparing a two-day fête and bazaar – a not
infrequent activity – she was, however, prevailed upon to draw the cover design
for the programme – the last of her artistic work reproduced in this volume.
The gathering in question was held under the patronage of the Emperor of
Ethiopia, the Ethiopian ambassador Dr. Martin, and, characteristic of her

general collective security stance, the ambassador of China. (*New Times and Ethiopia News* carried the occasional supplement entitled *China News*.) Working impromptu one Sunday without proper pen and ink, her writer's hands long unused to artistic activity, she drew two pigeons on a branch of a tree, with an Ethiopian cross and leaf border reminiscent of those in Ethiopian manuscript illuminations which she greatly admired (No. 90).

The outbreak of the Second World War in September 1939 was welcomed by *New Times and Ethiopia News* as putting an end to the appeasement period. (I remember early on the morning after Mr. Chamberlain's broadcast announcing the "state of war" with Germany that my mother was at work as usual in her office on the ground floor. My father, whose study was upstairs, happened to enter the room. Thereupon, I never knew quite why, she said they ought to have an "editorial meeting" – I had not heard of one before. She proceeded to observe that the paper, having always urged the need to resist the aggressors, would of course be wholehearted in supporting the Allied cause – but would at the same time continue its opposition to Mussolini who at that stage had not entered the conflict. To this my father assented without discussion, and the "editorial meeting" ended as abruptly as it had begun.) The newspaper, which then described itself as "The National Anti-Fascist Weekly", carried such slogans as "For Victory", "Fascism to Be Fought to a Finish", and "Restore to Independence All Nations Seized by the Aggressors".

My mother, recalling the difficulties which had afflicted so many people at the outset of the First World War and the callousness of slow-moving government bureaucracy, also helped to found a Women's War Emergency Council (established a week or so after the outbreak of war) to assist with various relief projects. Meetings were on occasion held at 64 Farringdon Street where she had some months earlier set up the New Times Bookshop which sold the paper and other literature, and held a series of gatherings, advertised as "Meet the Author Thursdays", at which writers gave brief talks and autographed copies of their books. The shop, the rent of which was always a struggle to meet, came to an end when the building, to my mother's relief, was destroyed in the London blitz.

The outbreak of the war affected her life in other ways too. With the beginning of hostilities the flow of Italian, Spanish, Basque, Jewish and other refugees, a succession of whom had stayed in our house before proceeding elsewhere, dried up and her home became quieter for a time. It was not long, however, before the German bombing began, and Woodford, lying on the bombers' route to London, suffered numerous air-raids, with the result that the family often spent night after night in the two tiny Anderson shelters dug in the garden. Another change in the household resulted from the fact that its mistress had been until then, on general humanitarian grounds, a vegetarian, but with the introduction of rationing – a system which she had advocated in the First World War and greatly praised on account of its fairness – she felt it "more practical" to turn to meat-eating like the population at large. Throughout this time she shopped as far as possible, as a matter of principle, at the Co-op of which she was a member.

The outbreak of hostilities moreover created new problems for her work, as the British government, embarrassed by a newspaper that continued to denounce fascist Italy – and might be an added irritant provoking the Duce into entering the European conflict – prohibited its export to neutral countries.

In June 1940 Mussolini, however, suddenly declared war on Britain and France. The news of this event, though expected for some months, created great excitement in our home. That Sunday, I recall, several Italian anti-Fascist refugees had come for dinner, as they often did at weekends, "for a plate of macaroni", and we turned on the BBC evening news after it had begun. The announcer was reading out some uninteresting news after which he proceeded to give a "fuller report of Signor Mussolini's declaration of war". These words struck guests and hosts like an electric shock which gave way to a feeling of relief, and hope for the future. The following issue of *New Times and Ethiopia News* carried a characteristic call to Italians written by my father, exclaiming:

> At last! The long agonising vigil is over.
> The Fascist enemy is today an open and declared enemy. . . . Mussolini
>   is the traitor, not we!
> To his call to arms, we answer: "Yes we shall fight, proud to do so, at
>   last – against you!
> "We shall avenge Matteotti, and Rosselli and the other victims of
>   your tyranny.
> "You have stolen the freedom of our native land; we shall re-conquer
>   it, arms in hand.
> "Ere long, by the side of the Allied forces, we shall enter victorious, in
>   Rome, free once more, and exact the punishment fitting for your
>   crimes.
> "We shall free the Italian name from the shame you have cast upon it."
> Hitler and Mussolini are now one: united in crime and dishonour they
>   shall fall together.

In the office of *New Times and Ethiopia News*, Woodford, 1940.

My mother was much concerned at this time with the question of enemy aliens in Britain. It came to her attention that many undoubtedly anti-Fascist Italians were being detained, while a number of leading Fascists, including some listed as such in directories, were left at large. She wrote many letters on the matter to the Home Office and sundry MPs, and publicised the matter in *New Times and Ethiopia News*. She received, as a result, a threatening letter from a London Fascist stating that her home would be bombed if she continued her agitation. The police, who seemed to have acted on false information, gradually put things right, though there was at least one irretrievable miscarriage of justice – the arrest of the anti-Fascist Angelo Crespi who died when the *Andorra Star,* the boat on which he was being taken to detention on the Isle of Man, was torpedoed by a German submarine. It was about this time, as we afterwards learned from the Press, that the Germans placed my mother's

The author in his study as a child, in 1940, reading a copy of his mother's newspaper. It reports Nazi and Fascist threats to her life.

name on the list of persons to be "arrested forthwith" in the event of a Nazi occupation of Britain.

As a result of Mussolini's entry into the European war the restrictions on foreign sales of *New Times and Ethiopia News* were immediately lifted. It still had, however, other crusades to fight, for the British government, bound by its previous recognition of the Italian empire and by colonialist prejudices, was slow to accord the Ethiopians the status of allies, and reluctant to allow the patriots what the latter considered adequate weaponry. In January 1941 British, Indian, South African and other Allied forces launched a two-pronged attack on the Italian East African empire from the Sudan in the west and Kenya in the south, while the Emperor, who had been flown out from Britain for the purpose, rallied Ethiopian refugees in the area to join hands with Ethiopian patriots in the country. Ethiopian participation in the struggle, though considered by my mother essential, was not so regarded in British official and colonial circles. She and her friends were instrumental in having a series of parliamentary questions raised in the House of Commons, and did constant battle with a prevaricating BBC which each Sunday broadcast the national anthems of the Allies and yet, making one excuse after another, continued to omit that of Ethiopia.[8] (It was not broadcast in fact until May 11, 1941, six days after the Emperor's re-entry into Addis Ababa.) She was subsequently in close contact with General Orde Wingate who allowed her to publish information he had given her on some of the problems he had encountered in the Ethiopian liberation campaign, not least with other commanders who wished victories to be achieved by British rather than Ethiopian arms.[9] The support of the British Royal Air Force for the patriots, he claimed, had for example been deliberately withdrawn in the later stages of the campaign, and orders given to halt the Emperor's advance, so that Addis Ababa should fall to South African rather than Ethiopian soldiers.

With the defeat of the Italian armies in East Africa in the spring of 1941 the newspaper acquired a new role – that of working for the liberation of Ethiopia from its liberators. The reason for this was that the country, though regarded by some as the "first to be freed" from Axis domination, was classed by the British military authorities as occupied enemy territory, the powers of the restored Ethiopian government were strictly curtailed and an extensive area of the country was kept under British occupation.

In 1942 the Emperor's daughter Princess Tsehai died. She was well known in Britain, having served as a nurse in London during the war, and had often spoken of her intention after the liberation of instituting a modern medical service in her country. My mother was persuaded, largely by my father, to respond to Tsehai's death by undertaking the hard work of raising funds to establish and equip the first modern hospital in Addis Ababa, which was to be named in the Princess's memory. The Princess Tsehai Memorial Hospital Council was duly established, under the patronage of the Emperor and Empress and their elder daughter, Princess Tenagne Work, with numerous distinguished members, including among them the Quaker educationalist Isabel Fry. The internationalist Lord Davies of Llandinam was chairman, and King George VI's personal physician, Lord Horder, was treasurer. Funds were collected from all over the world and my mother, as honorary secretary of the hospital council, made her first visit to Ethiopia in 1944 to assist in selecting the hospital site. (She tried to take me with her, but because of the war-time shipping shortage her request to the British authorities for this was turned down.) While in Ethiopia she met many old Ethiopian friends, and found that an Addis Ababa

Sylvia Pankhurst in Ethiopia, then recently liberated from Italian Fascist occupation, inspecting a modern printing press in 1944.

street had been named after her, and that one of the newly established Ethiopian newspapers had been called *Addis Zemen,* the Amharic translation of her *New Times.* She was not a little surprised to be awarded two Ethiopian medals, one of them the patriot's medal, with five palms, one for each year of the Fascist occupation. She broadcast from Radio Addis Ababa, visited many parts of the country, and described her journey in a series of articles in *New Times and Ethiopia News.* The country was then in a period of post-war reconstruction and many new institutions were being founded or re-established.

With the end of the European war in the following year, and the election of Clem Attlee's Labour government, of which she counted herself a supporter, she embarked upon what was to be her last major political campaign. This was concerned with the future of the former Italian colonies in Africa which was discussed first by the four great powers – Britain, France, the USA and the USSR – and later by the United Nations. One of the ex-colonies, Eritrea, which had been the springboard for Italian invasions of Ethiopia in 1894–5 and again in 1935–6, was from the historical and cultural point of view closely connected with that country, and many officials of the Ethiopian government, including

Outside the House of Commons in May 1948, Sylvia participates in a poster parade concerned with the disposal of former Italian colonies and the withdrawal of British troops from eastern Ethiopia. In front is the former Suffragette Mary Leigh; in the rear is the author.

Lorenzo Taezaz and Ephrem Tewelde Medhen, who had been among some of her closest Ethiopian friends during their exile in Britain, were in fact Eritrean. Union of the two territories, they and others argued, would moreover give Ethiopia greater security, as well as badly needed access to the sea. Many Eritreans were then clamouring for "reunion" to Ethiopia, and were being victimised for this by the British military administration of the territory. The alternative to reunion with Ethiopia at this stage seemed the return of Italian rule which had strong international backing, particularly from the Latin American countries. The editor of *New Times and Ethiopia News* who had been lobbied by Tedla Bairu and other Unionists while in Eritrea on her journey to Ethiopia in 1944,[10] was reinforced in her pro-Unionist views by the arrival for study in Britain of a number of Ethiopian students who included Habteab Bairu and other young Eritreans, all keen Unionists.

During this period Sylvia founded an International Ethiopian Council for Study and Report, published various pamphlets, including *Italy's War Crimes in Ethiopia* which contained an eye-witness account of the Graziani massacre of 1937 and was illustrated by gruesome photographs taken by the Italian Fascists of their own atrocities. She lobbied the twenty-one-power conference in Paris where the peace treaty with Italy was negotiated, held numerous meetings and conferences on the future of the former Italian colonies, and drafted letters to *The Times* and other journals, signed by such varied co-signatories as Lady Pethick Lawrence, Lady Dorothea Layton, the Deans of Gloucester and Winchester, the Socialist professor G.D.H.Cole and a number of MPs. She also wrote several books on Ethiopia and the ex-colonies: *The Ethiopian People: Their Rights and Progress* (1948), *Ex-Italian Somaliland* (1951), and *Eritrea on the Eve* (1952) which outlined the history of Ethiopia since the sixteenth-century. The latter work described the hideous conditions in the "native quarter" set aside for the indigenous population in the Eritrean capital, Asmara, and revealed the extent to which the British military administration had disposed of former Italian state property in the territory. This book was also issued as a pamphlet, entitled *Why are we destroying the Eritrean Ports?* In the following year appeared *Ethiopia and Eritrea: the Last Ten Years of the Reunion Struggle 1941–1951* which had an introduction by her old friend Emmeline Pethick Lawrence paying tribute to her work in the Suffragette movement. (My name also appeared on the title page, for my mother had suffered a heart attack one evening while rushing up the hill at Woodford to post "copy" from the main post office to her printer in Manchester – and I, then a student at the London School of Economics, helped by editing the work and writing some of the less important chapters. She soon recovered, however, and, to their dismay her doctor and some of her friends, shortly afterwards heard on the radio that the veteran Suffragette had spoken at a public demonstration held in Trafalgar Square to condemn South African apartheid.)

One of the Ethiopian students in whose education she took a close interest in this period was, perhaps significantly, Afewerk Tekle, a budding artist whose juvenile work she had been shown while inspecting his school during her visit to Ethiopia in 1944.

He arrived in London with two other schoolboys one week-end when the Ethiopian legation was closed and there was no one to meet him or arrange his accommodation. Asked at the airport if there was no one in England whom he knew, he recalled the English lady he had met at his school some years earlier. A call was put through to my mother who at once had me go to collect him and bring him home. It later transpired that he had been sent to England to study mining engineering, but, seeing his obvious artistic talents, she succeeded in persuading his government to allow him to transfer to art. She was made the official guardian of six Ethiopian students then studying in Britain, but fearing that the number would grow, later succeeded in getting the Ethiopian embassy in London to appoint an education attaché.

My mother undertook a second, more extensive visit to Ethiopia in 1951–2 (on which occasion I accompanied her for much of the time), and described the journey in a series of articles for her weekly newspaper. Around this time the paper organised exhibitions of Ethiopian produce, and tried, in collaboration with several British children's newspapers, to establish penfriendships between Ethiopian and other schoolchildren. Neither activity was much of a success, for Ethiopian exporters were not forthcoming to supply the products displayed, while the juvenile letters soon petered out. For the most part she refrained from involving herself in Ethiopia's internal affairs and, remembering the inefficiencies of British officialdom against which she had battled during World War I, took a patient view of the failings of the newly established Ethiopian bureaucracy. But she could not refrain from writing occasionally to the Ethiopian government to urge the desirability of establishing trade unions and cooperative societies, and when an agricultural cooperative was at last set up she gave it considerable publicity in her writings.

Her visit to Addis Ababa, the city which had been ravaged by the Fascists, and had been in sight of the Graziani massacre, inspired her to write an epic poem, *O Addis Ababa, O Fair New Flower*. Addressing the city, which had been founded towards the end of the nineteenth century by Emperor Menelik, she writes:

> *O Addis, in thy beauty named New Flower,*
> *Flanked by the Entoto Mountains and the plains*
> *Rendered so smiling by those tropic rains*
> *That bear to Egypt her perennial dower.*
> *Great Menelik did build thee for his bride,*
> *With fragrant Eucalyptus set thy ways*
> *And here St. George's silver dome did raise*
> *And there the Golden Lion, Judah's pride.*

Her artist's eye picks out some of the significant details of the street:

> *Faces of dusky loveliness, the gleam*
> *Of white teeth flashing in the engaging smile,*
> *Dark glistening eyes and lustrous – all the stream*
> *Of youth and happiness, the serried file*
> *Of merchants with their tropic wares, the spate*
> *Of mule trains plodding, camels laden high,*
> *Rolling like ships, with long and lurching gait*
> *And huge, split hooves, the desert traveller's mate;*

Sylvia speaking at a meeting held in London by the Princess Tsehai Memorial Hospital Council in 1950. On her right are two members of the council – Brigadier Parkinson and Lord Winster – and far left, the Ethiopian ambassador, Abebe Retta.

> *The splendid horsemen cantering, used well-nigh*
> *As centaurs to their steeds, erect and straight;*
> *And humble garries* with high driving seat,*
> *Looking but feather-weight, speed by so fleet.*

Remembering the eye-witness accounts of the three days of Fascist terror in 1937 she imagines the scene of "yet another hunt, another kill":

> *Unsated yet, the Fascio claims its fill*
> *Of blood, more blood, and harries on its hounds.*
> *The blackshirt braves these humble tukuls** soused*
> *With petrol; while the flames yet fiercer rise.*
> *Poor prisoned folk within raise toothless cries,*
> *And gloating gunmen wait to shoot them down.*
> *While shouts of "Duce!" still the murderers rouse*
> *A multitude seek ways to flee the town;*
> *Poor fugitives pursued by wheeling 'planes,*
> *They seek some hole, some refuge from these pains.*
> *Not the fierce torrent, nor the lion's den*
> *Could be so perilous as these wild men.*

---

* Two-wheeled, horse-drawn carriages.

** Traditional Ethiopian houses with thatched roofs.

A gathering of Ethiopian students at Leicester, 1950. Sylvia Pankhurst is front centre, the author, back row, fourth from right.

Alluding to earlier Italian attempts to colonise Ethiopia, which had been based on a diplomatic stratagem, she declares:

> *Not by a trick Ethiopia's antique fame*
> *Might like a spent torch die and leave no trace;*
> *Nor later by foul spray of poison gas*
> *Should end the freedom of the ancient race,*
> *Her age-old empire to oblivion pass,*
> *Not from the map be blotted out her name.*

Anxious to promote greater knowledge of the African country she had befriended, she wrote numerous articles on its history and culture, and produced a seven hundred page study *Ethiopia: A Cultural History*, which was published in 1955 with a preface by the orientalist churchman Canon John A. Douglas. It contained lengthy and at times perceptive descriptions of traditional Ethiopian art – which owed much to Byzantine influences – and with which she was greatly enamoured, as well as detailed accounts, based largely on her travels, of the antiquities of Aksum, the remarkable rock-hewn churches of Lalibela, and the notable seventeenth-century castles of Gondar.

In 1950 my father died,[11] in 1954, the hospital for which she had worked so hard was completed (a wing of it was given her name), and the British occupation of the last stretches of Ethiopia was fast drawing to a close. Seeing no further use for *New Times and Ethiopia News* my mother decided to accept

Sylvia (back centre) at the opening of the Princess Tsehai Memorial Hospital in Addis Ababa, July 1951. The Emperor is being shown round by the British director of the hospital, Colonel Byam.

Opposite: At London Airport, July 1, 1951, about to fly to Ethiopia where she was to spend the last years of her life. The author is in the background.

an earlier invitation from the Emperor to live in Ethiopia on a more permanent basis. She was then seventy-four years old.

Anticipating the beauties of the Ethiopian countryside, the mountains illuminated by the bright African sun, and expecting that she would at last have spare time on her hands she seems to have toyed with the idea of a limited return to art. Without saying much about it to me she took with her her old palette, and purchased several boxes of paints.

On arrival in Addis Ababa (having by now completed my studies, I went out with her to teach in the then University College of Addis Ababa) she was housed high above the city amid eucalyptus trees in one of the houses which had formed part of the old Italian legation. The building was then vacant as diplomatic relations between Ethiopia and Italy had not yet been resumed.

Sylvia Pankhurst at her son's wedding in Addis Ababa, 1957. Centre, Rita Pankhurst, in front, the two witnesses: left Ethiopian artist Afewerk Tekle, right, Ethiopian playwright Menghestu Lemma, both in national dress.

Later we moved to a bungalow, once again surrounded by eucalyptus trees, near the Princess Tsehai Memorial Hospital. (There my future wife Rita joined us to become a librarian at the National Library of Ethiopia. One of the two witnesses at our marriage, at the British Embassy in Addis Ababa, was Afewerk Tekle who had by then returned from his studies in Europe. The other witness was another Ethiopian former student in England, Menghestu Lemma, who had helped her with one of the chapters of *Ethiopia: A Cultural History*. The last four years of my mother's life, Rita and I spent with her in this house – together with an old white Persian cat she had brought with her from England.) At about this time she wrote to Elsa Fraenkel, an artist friend in Woodford, "you would love this country. The scenery is so beautiful and there are so many fine types who could serve as models for you."

Desirous of presenting a more comprehensive view of Ethiopia than had been possible in London she soon afterwards founded a monthly journal, *Ethiopia Observer*, which was published in Addis Ababa and London. Largely written by herself, it involved her in visits to numerous schools, hospitals and other institutions and historic sites, in some cases by Landrover to distant provinces. When once we remonstrated with her against taking a particularly arduous journey to a community school far off the beaten track, she replied,

Sylvia Pankhurst, editor of the *Ethiopia Observer*, on a reporting trip shortly before her death.

"Do you think my active life is over!"* She published special issues on a succession of topics, as for example the Addis Ababa town plan, the Ethiopian woman, industrial development, the Queen of Sheba and Pushkin's Ethiopian ancestry. (After her death, my wife and I were to continue the publication, as a quarterly, for a further fourteen years.)

She was soon much concerned at the extent of poverty in the Ethiopian capital, and particularly by the numerous disabled beggars. She would on occasion take a physically handicapped person from the street in her car, and have him operated on, at her expense, in the hospital. She later assisted in raising funds for an orthopaedic unit, and was instrumental in establishing the Social Service Society which attempted to run a rehabilitation centre in cooperation with the Addis Ababa municipality. The project had the enthusiastic support of the then reforming mayor of Addis Ababa, Dedjazmach Zawdie Gabre Selassie.

Once more at the publishing grindstone, and involved in continued fundraising for the Princess Tsehai Memorial Hospital, as well as for the newly

---

* She also flew on one occasion to Kenya (Rita and I accompanied her, as we did whenever we could) where she met Tom Mboya and other African nationalist leaders of the younger generation. (Her old friend Jomo Kenyatta was of course still in detention having been convicted of complicity in Mau Mau.)

established Social Service Society, she realised that her earlier hope of returning to her drawing had been no more than a dream. In a subsequent letter to Elsa Fraenkel she observed: "I often feel I should like to paint again in this beautiful country, but I am always busy and I feel that if I were to make a start I should be terribly disappointed with what I could produce after this interval of fifty years."

Towards the end of her life my mother received a letter from Elsa Fraenkel asking her to allow her to organise an exhibition of some of the pictures she had drawn almost half a century earlier. She somewhat reluctantly agreed, and accordingly wrote back: "If you like to make an exhibition for a few friends without expense ... there would be no objection, but do not try anything ambitious."

A small exhibition – the first public display of any of her work, other than that of the Prince's Skating Rink decorations, ever held – accordingly took place under the auspices of the Woman's Freedom League, the Suffragette Fellowship and the Royal India, Pakistan and Ceylon Society. It was opened at the French Institute in London, on December 15, 1959, by the then Indian High Commissioner, Mrs. Vijaya Lakshmi Pandit, who referred to the "remarkable talents" of an artist who had given up a promising career to join the Suffragette movement.

My mother wrote to Elsa Fraenkel thanking her for arranging the exhibition from what were "as it were, the ashes of fifty years ago", and, seeking to put her work in perspective, declared: "I gave up my work as an artist at twenty-seven years of age when I was just becoming efficient from the technical point of view".

Though, as she insisted, no longer herself an artist, she took a keen interest in the Ethiopian artistic scene, where modern artists were just beginning to emerge, helped to select paintings for an exhibition to go abroad, and watched in particular the career of Afewerk Tekle. She wrote to Elsa Fraenkel on July 3, 1960 – four months before her death: "I have persuaded him to get a model and do life drawing regularly; models here are so inexpensive and so beautiful! The scenery here is magnificent but one can hardly ever persuade him to leave the studio. I deeply regret being too old and busy for it. Such wonderful colour! Such wonderful costumes and people."

Though her creativity no longer found expression in art she continued to write poetry which she read regularly in her few moments of relaxation. After her death, we found in her notebook a poem, still in rough form, written after seeing a blind Ethiopian boy playing the piano, which began:

> *How did these blinkers fall on you of Ethiopian kind*
> *Whose eyes are strong and lustrous seeing far?*
> *Your shapely fingers touch the keys, ah welladay*
> *You sit entranced by your sweet melody.*

She had also begun a poem on the eucalyptus tree, which had soon after its importation from Australia at the end of the nineteenth-century become the dominant feature of the Addis Ababa landscape:

> *O lofty, lofty eucalyptus tree*
> *Bowing your dusky crests to every breeze*
> *How upright in your serried ranks you stand*
> *As did your forebears in th'Australian land*
> *Fair island in the far antipodes.*
> *Welcome you are, for your strong speedy growth*
> *Endears you to the thrifty peasant wife.*
> *Your numerous stems forever give men life.*

Living as she did amid eucalyptus trees she noted:

> *And when the monsoon shakes you how you sway*
> *Creaking and groaning, while it tears away*
> *Your rod-like strips of bark and hurls them far.*

She was saddened to see the harvesting of these trees, which were cut down every ten years or so to supply the capital with building material and fire wood, and continued:

You are gone my Eucalyptus woods that I have watched so gladly in your many changing moods. The woodman's axe has brought you to the ground. Only poor stumps remain of your once serried files of stately growths and those high gracious holding crests that bowed all gloriously to every wind.

> *More lovely than your far Australian kind,*
> *Those conquerors from whom your seed were sprung,*
> *So you are gone poor victims of the axe.*
> *Yet from your death your life shall rise again,*
> *A single stem replaced by four or five.*
> *While yet your root remains you are alive,*
> *Like Phoenix!*[12]

She died in Addis Ababa on September 27, 1960, at the age of seventy-eight. It

Sylvia Pankhurst's desk in Addis Ababa after her death.

was the festival of Masqal* when the rainy season draws to an end. The myriad yellow daisies which carpet the Ethiopian mountains at this time, and which she loved so much, were in full bloom.

She was buried in the Selassie, or "Trinity" cathedral, in ground set aside for the patriots whose struggles for Ethiopian independence and unity she had shared.[13] The name Sylvia being unknown to the Ethiopian Orthodox Church, she, though an unwavering agnostic throughout her life, was interred as Walata Krestos, or "daughter of Christ", in the presence of a large congress of mourners which included the Emperor, as well as many other Ethiopian friends old and new.

---

* One of the principal holidays of the Ethiopian year, celebrating the discovery of the True Cross by Saint Helena.

SOURCES

CHAPTER 1

1 E.S.Pankhurst, *The Suffragette Movement: An Intimate Account of Persons and Ideas.* London, 1931, p. 58.

2 *Ibid.,* p. 3.

3 The Countess of Oxford and Asquith, *Myself When Young by Famous Women of Today.* London, 1938, pp. 260–1.

4 *The Suffragette Movement,* p. 58.

5 C. Pankhurst, *Unshackled: The Story of How We Won the Vote.* London, 1959, p. 24.

6 *Myself When Young,* p. 262.

7 A.Pryce-Jones, *Little Innocents.* London, 1932, p. 38.

8 *The Suffragette Movement,* p. 88.

9 *Little Innocents,* p. 39.

10 *The Suffragette Movement,* p. 91.

11 *Ibid.,* pp. 103–4.

12 *Ibid.,* pp. 104–5.

13 *Ibid.,* pp. 106–7.

14 *Ibid.,* p. 107.

15 E.S.Pankhurst, *The Suffragette: The History of the Women's Militant Suffrage Movement 1905–1910.* London, 1911, p. 5.

16 *Myself When Young,* p. 264.

17 *The Suffragette Movement,* pp. 107–8.

18 *Ibid.,* p. 99.

19 *Myself When Young,* p. 267.

20 *The Suffragette Movement,* p. 105.

21 *Ibid.,* p. 110.

22 *Ibid.,* p. 111.

23 *Myself When Young,* p. 265.

CHAPTER 2

1 *The Suffragette Movement,* p. 114.

2 *Ibid.,* p. 122.

3 *Ibid.,* pp. 125–6.

4 *Ibid.,* p. 126.

5 *Ibid.,* p. 146.

6 *Ibid.,* p. 155.

CHAPTER 3

1 *The Suffragette Movement,* p. 160.

2 *Ibid.,* pp. 160–1.

3 *Ibid.,* pp. 161–3.

4 *Ibid.,* p. 163; *Unshackled,* p. 43.

5 *The Suffragette Movement,* p. 165.

CHAPTER 4

1 *The Suffragette Movement,* p. 171.

2 *Ibid.,* p. 218.

3 *Ibid.,* pp. 173–4.

4 *Myself When Young,* p. 278.

5 *The Suffragette Movement,* p. 178.

6 *The Suffragette,* p. 11.

7 *The Suffragette Movement,* p. 184.

CHAPTER 5

1 *The Suffragette Movement,* p. 193.

2 G. Salvemini, *Prelude to World War II.* London, 1953, p. 108.

3 *The Suffragette Movement,* p. 197.

4 E.Pethick Lawrence, *My Part in a Changing World.* London, 1938, pp. 147–9; see also A.Kenney, *Memories of a Militant.* London, 1924, p. 59.

5 *The Suffragette,* pp. 57–8.

6 *Ibid.,* p. 70.

7 *Ibid.,* pp. 79–80.

8 *Ibid.,* p. 91.

9 *The Suffragette Movement,* pp. 221–2.

10 *Myself When Young,* pp. 284–5.

CHAPTER 6

1 *The Suffragette*, pp. 104–5.
2 *Ibid.*, pp. 109–10.
3 *Ibid.*, pp. 111–16.
4 *Ibid.*, pp. 121–2.
5 *The Daily News.* November 7, 1907.
6 *The Suffragette Movement*, p. 240.
7 *The Suffragette*, pp. 139–40.
8 *Votes for Women.* 1909, p. 250.

CHAPTER 7

1 *The Suffragette Movement*, p. 261.
2 *Ibid.*, pp. 261–2.
3 *The Suffragette*, p. 158.
4 *The Suffragette Movement*, p. 263.
5 E.S.Pankhurst, "Pit-Brow Women," *Votes for Women.* 1911, p. 730.
6 *Myself When Young*, p. 289.
7 *Ibid.*, pp. 289–90.
8 *The Suffragette Movement*, pp. 270–1.
9 E.S.Pankhurst, "Women Farm Labourers in the Border Counties," *Votes for Women.* 1910, pp. 776–7.
10 E.S.Pankhurst, "The Potato-Pickers," *Votes for Women.* 1908, p. 294.
11 *The Suffragette Movement*, p. 271; *Myself When Young*, p. 291.
12 Letter to Elsa Fraenkel. December 5, 1959.
13 *The Suffragette Movement*, p. 271; see also *Myself When Young*, p. 291.
14 *The Suffragette Movement*, p. 272; see also *The Suffragette*, p. 98.

CHAPTER 8

1 *The Suffragette*, p. 242.
2 *Ibid.*, pp. 242–4.
3 *The Suffragette Movement*, p. 284.
4 *The Suffragette*, pp. 245, 248, 251.
5 *Ibid.*, pp. 283–4.
6 *Ibid.*, p. 339.

7 *The Suffragette Movement*, p. 218.
8 *Votes for Women.* 1908, p. 2.
9 *Ibid.*, 1908, p. 270.
10 *The Suffragette Movement*, p. 218.
11 *Votes for Women.* 1908, p. 472.
12 *The Suffragette*, p. 400.
13 *Ibid.*, pp. 398–400; see also *The Suffragette Movement*, p. 310.
14 *The Suffragette Movement*, p. 218.
15 Letter to Elsa Fraenkel. August 7, 1959.
16 *The Suffragette Movement*, pp. 304–5.
17 *The Suffragette*, pp. 374–5.
18 *The Suffragette Movement*, p. 305.

CHAPTER 9

1 *The Suffragette Movement*, p. 316; see also G.Dangerfield, *The Strange Death of Liberal England.* London, 1966, p. 175.
2 *Myself When Young*, p. 295.
3 *The Suffragette Movement*, p. 320.
4 Letter to Elsa Fraenkel. August 18, 1959.
5 Letters to National Portrait Gallery. February 14, 1956, and August 24, 1959.
6 *The Suffragette Movement*, p. 335; see also Kenney, *op. cit.*, pp. 152–3.
7 *The Suffragette Movement*, pp. 345–6.
8 *Ibid.*, p. 350.
9 Letter to Elsa Fraenkel. August 7, 1959.
10 *Ibid.*
11 *The Suffragette Movement*, pp. 354–5.
12 *Votes for Women.* 1911, pp. 135, 155, 169.
13 *The Suffragette Movement*, p. 372.
14 *Ibid.*, p. 384.
15 *Ibid.*, p. 386.
16 E.S.Pankhurst, "Mrs. Pankhurst's Birthday," *Votes for Women.* July 12, 1912.
17 *Votes for Women.* July 19, 1912.
18 *The Suffragette Movement*, p. 394.
19 *Ibid.*, p. 383.

CHAPTER 10

1 *The Suffragette Movement*, p. 396.

2 *The Suffragette*. February 28, 1913.

3 *The Suffragette Movement*, p. 402.

4 *Ibid.*, p. 413.

5 *Ibid.*, pp. 416–17.

6 *Ibid.*, p. 417.

7 *Ibid.*, p. 428; see also G.Lansbury, *Looking Backwards – and Forwards*. London, 1935; and R.Postgate, *The Life of George Lansbury*. London, 1951, p. 120.

8 *The Suffragette Movement*, p. 432.

9 *Ibid.*, p. 445.

10 *The Suffragette Movement*, pp. 469–70.

11 *The Suffragette Movement*, p. 475.

12 *Ibid.*, p. 495.

13 *Ibid.*, p. 498.

14 *Ibid.*, pp. 502–3; see also Dangerfield, *op. cit.*, pp. 315, 353.

CHAPTER 11

1 *The Suffragette Movement*, pp. 517–19; see also Dangerfield, *op. cit.*, pp. 203–4, 354.

2 *Votes for Women*. February 13, 1914.

3 *The Suffragette Movement*, p. 540.

4 *Ibid.*, p. 566.

5 W.H.Nevinson, *More Changes, More Chances*. London, 1925, p. 320.

6 *Ibid.*, p. 337.

7 Pethick Lawrence, *op. cit.*, pp. 304–5.

8 Dangerfield, *op. cit.*, p. 350.

9 Letter to Elsa Fraenkel, August 7. 1959.

10 *Myself When Young*, pp. 311–12.

11 Pethick Lawrence, *op. cit.*, p. 150.

12 Letter to Elsa Fraenkel. December 5, 1959.

13 E.S.Pankhurst, *The Home Front*. London, 1932. p. 330.

14 *The Home Front*, pp. 72, 427.

CHAPTER 12

1 E.S.Pankhurst, *Writ on Cold Slate*. London, 1921, pp. 5, 7, 9, 17, 20, 21, 22, 23.

2 E.S.Pankhurst, *Poems of Mihail Eminescu*. London, 1930, pp. 39–65.

3 R.J.Pankhurst, "The Library of Emperor Tewodros II and Maqdala (Magdala)," *Bulletin of the School of Oriental and African Studies*. 1973, Vol. XXXV, Part 1, pp. 15–22.

4 D.Whaley, *British Public Opinion and the Abyssinian War 1935–6*. London, 1975.

5 G.Padmore, *Pan-Africanism or Communism?* London, 1956, *passim*; Ras Makonnen, *Pan-Africanism from Within*, edited by Kenneth King. London, 1973, *passim*.

6 R.Pankhurst, "Emperor Haile Selassie's Litigation in England to Reassert the Independence of Ethiopia during the Italian Occupation in 1937 and 1938," *Ethiopia Observer*. 1971, Vol. XIV, No. 1, pp. 3–10.

7 A.Del Boca, *The Ethiopian War 1935–1941*. Chicago, 1969, *passim*; A.Mockler, *Il mito dell' impero*. Milano, 1977, *passim*.

8 R.Pankhurst, "The Ethiopian National Anthem in 1940," *Ethiopia Observer*. 1971, Vol. XIV, No. 3, pp. 219–25; *idem*, "The Ethiopian National Anthem in 1941," 1972, Vol. XV, No. 1, pp. 63–6.

9 C.Sykes, *Orde Wingate*. London, 1959, *passim*.

10 E.S. and R.K.P.Pankhurst, *Ethiopia and Eritrea*. Woodford Green, Essex, 1952, pp. 95–113.

11 *New Times and Ethiopia News*. January 23, 1954.

12 *Ethiopia Observer*. 1961, Vol. V, No. 1, p. 25.

13 *Ethiopia Observer*. 1961, Vol. V, No. 1, pp. 43–9.

DETAILS OF WORKS

BLACK AND WHITE ILLUSTRATIONS

No. 1: $11\frac{7}{8}$in × $19\frac{3}{8}$in (30.3cm × 49.2cm). Watercolour with touches of Prussian blue ink on white paper.

No. 2: 11in × 19in (27.9cm × 48.3cm). Watercolour.

No. 3: $10\frac{3}{8}$in × 9in (26.5cm × 22.8cm). Watercolour, coloured ink and gold paint on white watercolour paper.

No. 4: $8\frac{7}{8}$in × $10\frac{1}{2}$in (22.5cm × 26.8cm). Watercolour heightened with coloured ink on rough surface watercolour paper.

No. 5: 7in × $9\frac{7}{8}$in (17.7cm × 25.2cm). Watercolour and coloured ink on watercolour paper.

No. 6: $6\frac{1}{2}$in × $11\frac{3}{8}$in (16.5cm × 28.8cm). Watercolour on rough surface white watercolour paper.

No. 7: $8\frac{1}{2}$in × $11\frac{3}{4}$in (21.8cm × 29.8cm). Watercolour with touches of gouache and coloured ink on pale buff paper.

No. 8: $14\frac{3}{4}$in × $23\frac{7}{8}$in (37.5cm × 60.5cm). Oil on white-primed canvas.

No. 10: $14\frac{5}{8}$in × $10\frac{1}{2}$in (37.1cm × 26.7cm). Watercolour.

No. 12: 1905. Pen and ink.

No. 16: Approx. $13\frac{1}{8}$in × $17\frac{3}{4}$in (33.5cm × 45cm). Charcoal on white surface paper.

No. 17: $10\frac{7}{8}$in × $15\frac{1}{8}$in (27.5cm × 38.5cm). Gouache and watercolour on greenish-grey paper.

No. 18: $10\frac{5}{8}$in × 17in (27cm × 43cm). Gouache and watercolour on pale greenish paper.

No. 19: $13\frac{1}{8}$in × 20in (33.5cm × 50.9cm). Gouache and watercolour on dark brown paper.

No. 20: $12\frac{1}{2}$in × $16\frac{3}{8}$in (31.8cm × 41.8cm). Charcoal and gouache on white cartridge paper.

No. 21: 11in × $13\frac{3}{8}$in (28cm × 34cm). Charcoal on white paper.

No. 22: $18\frac{1}{4}$in × $13\frac{1}{2}$in (46.3cm × 34.2cm). Gouache and watercolour on a mid-toned blue-grey cartridge paper.

No. 23: $7\frac{1}{2}$in × $11\frac{1}{8}$in (19cm × 28.4cm). Gouache and watercolour on blue-grey watercolour paper.

No. 24: $10\frac{7}{8}$in × $16\frac{3}{4}$in (27.5cm × 42.4cm), Gouache and watercolour on pale buff paper.

No. 42: $9\frac{3}{4}$in × $14\frac{5}{8}$in (24.8cm × 37.2cm). Watercolour over pencil drawing.

No. 43: $26\frac{1}{8}$in × $20\frac{1}{8}$in (66.4cm × 51.1cm). Red, white and black chalk.

No. 44: $18\frac{3}{4}$in × $23\frac{7}{8}$in (46.8cm × 60.7cm). Red, white and black chalk on olive grey paper. Dated 1910, this is the only work to carry a date.

No. 45: $16\frac{1}{4}$in × $22\frac{1}{8}$in (41.2cm × 56.3cm). Red, white and black chalk on buff-coloured paper.

No. 46: $22\frac{1}{4}$in × $16\frac{3}{4}$in (56.5cm × 42.5cm). Charcoal, white chalk and red crayon.

No. 47: 7in × 10in (17.7cm × 25.4cm). Watercolour and gouache on white watercolour paper.

Nos. 48–57: From a sketchbook. Pencil and watercolour.

Nos. 58–63: From a sketchbook. Watercolour.

Nos. 64–89: Watercolour.

COLOUR PLATES

Plate I: $11\frac{3}{4}$in × $16\frac{3}{4}$in (28.8cm × 42.6cm). Gouache and watercolour on brown ochre paper.

Plate II: $10\frac{1}{8}$in × 7in (25.6cm × 17.7cm). Gouache on watercolour paper.

Plate III: $10\frac{1}{4}$in × $16\frac{1}{4}$in (26cm × 41.4cm). Gouache and watercolour on coloured paper.

Plate IV: $12\frac{7}{8}$in × $20\frac{1}{8}$in (32.7cm × 51cm). Gouache and watercolour on white watercolour paper

Plate V: $10\frac{3}{4}$in × $16\frac{3}{4}$in (27.4cm × 42.4cm). Gouache and watercolour on brown paper.

Plate VI: $13\frac{1}{2}$in × $17\frac{3}{8}$in (34.4cm × 44.2cm). Red, black and white chalk on olive grey paper.

Plate VII: $12\frac{3}{4}$in × $17\frac{7}{8}$in (33.5cm × 45.6cm). Gouache and watercolour on olive brown paper.

Plate VIII: $13\frac{1}{8}$in × 18in (33.5cm × 45.6cm). Gouache and watercolour on dark brown paper.

Plate IX: $9\frac{7}{8}$in × $11\frac{1}{4}$in (25cm × 28.6cm).

Plate X: $10\frac{1}{2}$in × $5\frac{1}{8}$in (25.8cm × 13cm). Gouache and watercolour on brown ochre cartridge paper.

Plate XI: $12\frac{1}{2}$in × $8\frac{7}{8}$in (31.8cm × 22.5cm). Gouache and watercolour on brown paper.

Plate XII: 11in × $16\frac{7}{8}$in (28cm × 43cm). Gouache and watercolour on grey paper.

Plate XIII: $3\frac{3}{4}$in × $4\frac{3}{4}$in (9.5cm × 12.1cm). Colour-printed reproduction of gouache design.

Plate XIV: $11\frac{7}{8}$in × 16in (30.3cm × 40.6cm). Red, black and white chalk on olive grey paper.

Plate XV: $16\frac{1}{8}$in × $22\frac{1}{8}$in (41cm × 56.2cm). Red, black and white chalk on buff-coloured paper.

Plate XVI: $9\frac{7}{8}$in × $13\frac{7}{8}$in (25.1cm × 35.3cm). Oil on linen canvas.

HE THAT GOETH
FORTH and WEEPETH

BEARING
PRECIOUS SEED

SHALL DOUBTLESS
COME